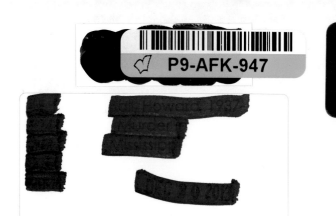

Murder in Mississippi

LANDMARK LAW CASES

&

AMERICAN SOCIETY

Peter Charles Hoffer

N. E. H. Hull

Series Editors

HOWARD BALL

Murder in Mississippi

United States v. Price

and the Struggle for Civil Rights

UNIVERSITY PRESS OF KANSAS

Published by the University Press of Kansas (Lawrence, Kansas 66049), which was organized by the Kansas Board of Regents and is operated and funded by Emporia State University, Fort Hays State University, Kansas State University, Pittsburg State University, the University of Kansas, and Wichita State University

Library of Congress Cataloging-in-Publication Data

Ball, Howard, 1937–
Murder in Mississippi : United States v. Price and the struggle for civil rights / Howard Ball.
  p. cm. — (Landmark law cases & American society)
Includes bibliographical references and index.
ISBN 0-7006-1315-3 (cloth : alk. paper) — ISBN 0-7006-1316-1 (pbk. : alk. paper)
  1. Trials (Murder) — Mississippi. 2. Murder — Mississippi — Neshoba County — History — 20th century. 3. Civil rights workers — Crimes against — Mississippi — Neshoba County — History — 20th century. 4. Goodman, Andrew, 1943–1964. 5. Chaney, James Earl, 1943–1964. 6. Schwerner, Michael Henry, 1939–1964. I. Title. II. Series.

KF224.M47B35   2004
345.73′02523′09762 — dc22   2003024026

British Library Cataloguing-in-Publication Data is available.

Printed in the United States of America

10 9 8 7 6 5 4 3 2

The paper used in this publication meets the minimum requirements of the American National Standard for Permanence of Paper for Printed Library Materials z39.48-1984.

Dedicated to my grandchildren
Lila Jules Bernhardt and
Nathan Asher Bernhardt,
and to Carol

CONTENTS

Every book in the Landmark Law Cases series is exceptional in some fashion. Howard Ball's remarkable account of the June 21, 1964, murder of three civil rights workers in the heartland of the Ku Klux Klan and the trials that followed certainly fits this description. Although the events led to a decision by the United States Supreme Court, and there were important issues of federal criminal jurisdiction at stake, the opinion of the Court did not concern itself with artificial or arcane reasoning. Its opinion in *United States v. Price et al.*, 1966, like Ball's book itself, is about people, some courageous and others despicable; about crime, injustice, official malfeasance, compromise, and politics. But this in itself does not make Ball's work different from other titles in the series.

The crime took place in Philadelphia, Mississippi, during one of the "Freedom Summers" of the early 1960s. With the eyes of the nation focused on them, idealistic young people from all over the country joined civil rights workers from Mississippi to register black voters. Violence against the voters went back to Reconstruction. Violence against "outsiders" was just as old and just as ingrained in the culture of the Deep South. While many — perhaps most — whites wanted an end to the violence and saw its injustice, many not only condoned it but participated. The murders of two white, Jewish New Yorkers and one African American Mississippian should have been quickly solved by local authorities, were not they involved in the homicidal conspiracy themselves. Federal indictments of the men identified by the FBI as the murderers were thrown out by a federal district court judge. Two years later he was overturned by the U.S. Supreme Court. The subsequent trial, in federal court, led to the conviction of seven Klansmen. But as remarkable as these events were, they do not explain why this book is different.

The story itself is galvanizing, and Ball tells it in fast-paced and engaging fashion. Through interviews, documentary and archival evidence, and trial records, he uncovers the plotting of the conspirators and the planning of their prosecutors. What is more, he roots it in the long struggle for racial justice in Mississippi. Thus we learn about Mississippi's White Citizens Council (WCC) and the Sovereignty

Commission, whose members labored to prevent desegregation in the state, as well as about the civil rights, student, and church groups that targeted Mississippi for years before the murders. We follow the politicians in Washington, D.C., who tried to dodge the issue and the reactionary ones in Mississippi who looked for ways to deny equality to one half of their citizens. We meet a federal judge determined to undermine the rule of law who got angry and changed his mind in the middle of a trial and a solicitor general of the United States who never wavered in his determination to enforce the law. This book is fascinating and compelling reading. But all this is not what makes *Murder in Mississippi* so singular.

Ball taught in Mississippi for many years when the events were fresh in the memories of whites and blacks. He experienced firsthand the unfulfilled dreams of justice and the feral prejudices of Mississippians. Using this special perspective, he moves back and forth in time, weaving the tales of the victims and the perpetrators into a single tapestry. This is the stuff of classic tragedy, and also of catharsis, as Ball follows the principals' lives into the millennium. In these pages we come to feel as well as know the dangers and the triumphs of the civil rights movement. Seen in this new light, the legal process becomes political and personal, as close to the protagonists and, through Ball's efforts, to us as battle is to combat soldiers. And this makes Ball's work such a special and worthy part of the Landmark series.

ACKNOWLEDGMENTS

First of all, I have to thank Mike Briggs, the Editor in Chief of the University Press of Kansas, for his friendship and his astute guidance. It is always a pleasure to work with him and his wonderful staff at the Press. Thanks also to Peter Hoffer, one of the editors of this series, for his very helpful suggestions and his encouragement.

Many archivists have helped me with this project — and with others I have tackled in the past three-plus decades of research and scholarship in the areas of public law and civil rights and liberties. Dr. David Hilliard, the Director of the Mississippi History and Archives Center in Jackson, Mississippi, and his experienced staff provided me with the necessary assistance to navigate the Mississippi State Sovereignty Commission files. Dr. David Wigdor, the Assistant Director of the Manuscripts Division at the Library of Congress, and his excellent staff have been invaluable to me in my research activities in Washington, D.C., for at least the past twenty years. In my travels to many archives, I have always been impressed with the dedication and creativity of these wonderful people. This is another opportunity to thank them all for their excellent work over these many years.

A number of people assisted me in the research for this book and taught me a great deal about the demons and angels residing in Mississippi now — and in the past. This is the appropriate place for me to thank them for their help and friendship.

Donna Ladd, a fine writer and a former student of mine when I taught at Mississippi State University in the 1970s, has assisted me in many ways. Donna grew up in Philadelphia, Mississippi, and — through friendships with their young children or nieces and nephews — knew most of the Klansmen involved in the murders of the civil rights workers in 1964. She provided me with shelter when I visited Jackson, Mississippi, in June 2002 to work in the Mississippi State Archives on the recently released Mississippi State Sovereignty Commission files. She also shared with me some of her research findings, especially the essays of Bill Minor, a veteran journalist who has observed the goings-on in Mississippi for almost fifty years. Her essay "Unfinished Business: Mississippi Struggles with Racist Past and Present," completed as part of her master's degree work at Columbia University's School of Journalism, provided me — through her interviews — with insights into the minds of two young Mississippi lawyers, Ken Tucker, Neshoba County's district attorney, and Mike Moore, Mississippi's attorney general. They are both very committed to bringing to justice the Klansmen who were involved in the execution of the three civil rights workers, Mickey Schwerner, J. E. Chaney, and Andy Goodman, the evening of June 21–22, 1964.

Another former student of mine at MSU is Sid Salter, the present-day features editor at the *Jackson Clarion-Ledger.* He, too, grew up in Philadelphia, Mississippi, and knew the men who killed the three civil rights workers. He — like Donna — went to public school with many of their children. From his perspective as a newspaper publisher and editor, he gave me insights into the minds of Neshoba County residents, including some information about his cousin — one of five defense counsel for the Neshoba County Klansmen during their October 1967 conspiracy trial in federal district court in Meridian, Mississippi. He also shared with me some data and books he has collected over the years.

Beyond all else, these connections with former Mississippi students were immensely rewarding. Both of them have been fighting ceaselessly for fair justice in a state where both words — until recently — were invisible. They believe that until justice is achieved in the case of the murdered civil rights workers, the state will remain mired in the ugliness of the past.

Two dear friends from my six-year residency in Mississippi — and beyond those years to the present — are Charles and Suzie Lowery. Charles, a historian, taught at MSU for many years, as well as serving as the university's Associate Dean of the College of Arts and Sciences. Suzie and I served on the board of directors of the predominantly black Starkville Industrial Day Care Center, where I saw firsthand how persistent and evil institutionalized racism can be in a rural, southern setting. Both taught the "street kid" from the Bronx a great deal about country living in the Deep South, especially what 'possums look like and how they behave. Both have been fighters for social justice wherever they have resided.

Bill Giles, a wonderful colleague from the Department of Political Science at MSU, also guided me in my journey across Mississippi. Bill grew up in Louisiana and in many ways has never left New Orleans. He is a master chef and wise beyond his years in the ways of southern politicians and the fabled southern heritage. He was my mentor when, as the new Head of the Department of Political Science at the university, I had to instantly become familiar with what was for me a totally unfamiliar area of my discipline, public administration. In his travels with me across the state, I was able to learn many things about Mississippians that were not written down in textbooks. He also was the first person I knew who was dedicated to maintenance of our environment—long before that issue became an important public policy matter.

I will always cherish the memory of two other men, both southerners: Jim McComas and Bill Collins. Jim was the incoming President of MSU when my family arrived in Starkville, Mississippi, in July 1976. For as long as we worked together, he was a staunch champion of civil and human rights for all persons. As President, he shielded me from the venom contained in many dozens of letters and calls for my "firing" because of my very visible activities with the Voting Section of the U.S. Department of Justice and with the state's small American Civil Liberties Union affiliate. Only when I was leaving MSU in 1982 did I find out how he had handled the numerous condemnations of my professional work. Jim and his wife lovely wife, Adele, moved to other academic venues until his early death from pancreatic cancer. He, too, was my mentor in the ways of academic politics. I still cherish the correspondence we had after I was appointed, in 1984, Dean of the College of Social and Behavioral Science at the University of Utah.

Bill Collins is the other person whose presence had a dramatic impact on my development as a person and an academic administrator. One of the founders of the National Association of Schools of Public Affairs and Administration (NASPAA) in 1977, Bill came to MSU a year after me as the Director of the newly established John C. Stennis Center for Public Affairs. He, too, like the others I have mentioned here, was a fighter for social justice in the South. He had been a major figure in Georgia, running the University of Georgia's Local Government Institute for over two decades before coming to Mississippi in 1977. He and I also shared something else; we were born, twenty years apart, on the same day, August 13. He used the facilities of the Stennis Center to provide all Mississippians with important information about the meaning of democracy, tolerance, diversity, and social justice. I fondly remember him handling a phone call from Senator John Stennis after an op-ed piece of mine was published in the

Washington Post. The senator was livid, for evidently another senator, Ted Kennedy, had read portions of my piece on the floor of the Senate. The reasons: in addition to my very strong support in the op-ed piece for the extension, in 1982, of the 1965 Voting Rights Act, I was speaking as a member of the faculty at Mississippi State University—Stennis's alma mater! Well, the distinguished senator wanted me fired for my views. And it was Bill Collins who gently but persuasively reminded the senator from DeKalb, Mississippi, of the primacy of the First Amendment and academic freedom. Bill's effervescent wife, Mayzie, was a unique delight and continually "woke up" the denizens of Starkville, Mississippi. Bill Collins, who also succumbed to cancer, will forever be a part of who I am.

Two other individuals, although born above the Mason-Dixon Line, resided in the South for a long time and have been constant friends and colleagues since at least 1966. Thomas Lauth, the first Dean of the new School of Public and International Affairs (SPIA) at the University of Georgia, has lived in Georgia since 1967 and has taught both at Georgia State University and, since the mid-1970s, at the University of Georgia in Athens. He and his lovely wife, Jean, have been close friends since our first teaching job at Hofstra University in the mid-1960s. Many a cold wintry day did we drive into Hofstra from Suffolk County with the windows wide open in Tom's car because of exhaust fumes leaking into the vehicle. Tom is another transplanted northerner who—along with his wife—has continuously addressed the problem of racial intolerance whether found in church, in government, or on campus.

Phillip Cooper is my other constant colleague. He, too, taught at Georgia State and was a colleague of Tom's in the political science department there. He, too, reacted bitterly to the racism he saw around him in the city of Atlanta, the city "too busy to hate." After years of dealing with the dilemma, he left the South and has never returned. He and I are now colleagues at the University of Vermont, where he is the Distinguished Gund Professor of Liberal Arts in the College of Arts and Sciences. He and his wife, Claudia, continue to battle the demons of racism, across the nation and beyond as they continue their research on the plight of refugees internationally.

Many others have met the challenge of the racism—and the racists—in America. Responding to racism is not like playing tiddledywinks; there were many nights in Mississippi when my wife, Carol, picked up the telephone only to hear the loud bleats of racists on the other end of the line. However, for my colleagues and friends, there simply was no other choice but to confront these abhorrent realities.

Finally, there is my life companion, my wife, Carol. She, too, has seen the evil of racism and intolerance, in Mississippi and elsewhere, and she, too, has responded vigorously to these ugly people and situations. For more than forty years she has accompanied me in trying to better the society we found ourselves in — failing and succeeding in equal amounts. I cannot thank her or my three daughters and their husbands — Susan, Sheryl and Jay, and Melissa and Patrick — enough for their forbearance during the past decades.

Thank you all, including my four-legged companions — Sam, Maggie, Charlie, Stormin' Norman, Smokey, and Dirty Harry — for your love, your insights, your goodwill, your wet kisses, and your strength in the face of some pretty tough situations. As we say in Covarrubius, Spain: "Vaya con dios."

Murder in Mississippi

INTRODUCTION

It is the 1976–1977 baseball year at Mississippi State University. Two of us in the university's Department of Political Science attend a ballgame between Mississippi and the University of Florida. We sit in the bleachers, the next to last row. Behind us are five local Starkville, Mississippi, residents, who sit in the last row in order to expel the juice from their chewing tobacco over the side. The Florida team has a black center fielder, and the quintet constantly harangue the young man, hurling all kinds of racial epithets at him.

About the fifth inning or thereabouts, the Florida player comes to bat again, and the boys behind us start up again with their taunts. By this time my colleague has had it. He stands up, turns toward the group, and yells at them, calling them Klansmen and telling them to shut up. He immediately sits down. I quickly turn to him and say, full of fear, "Do you want to get us killed by these guys?" Before my colleague can answer, I feel a hard tap on my back. Turning, I look into the face of the closest John Deere hat. He says, "Ten years ago, we woulda killed your buddy, but times have changed. If'n your friend says one more word, we'll hafta throw him off the bleachers!" The two of us move quickly to seats closer to the field.

Times change — ever so slowly in some places — but they do change. Ten years earlier, in Starkville, Mississippi, and in every other city and town in the Magnolia State, the third incarnation of the Ku Klux Klan was at its peak. Thousands of white Mississippians had left the cozy confines of the White Citizens Council for the more violent, more terrifying Mississippi KKK.

A decade earlier, no one but a crazy person would have cursed at and told a Klansman to shut up. There was across the state a pervasive fear of the Klan by the good folk of Mississippi. If they were repelled or repulsed by the Klan's behavior — and many thousands were — they remained silent for fear of the consequences of speaking out against these violent men. The fellow who spoke to me was probably right; if my colleague had uttered those words in public in 1966, he probably would have been paid a bloody visit by members of the local Klavern that very night. Instead, a decade later, in 1976, he might have just "fallen" from the bleachers. Times change!

Murder in Mississippi recounts a story that takes place in that earlier frightening, fearful time before change in American history. Most Mississippians remained silent during the time of the third Klan, 1963–1970. Very few persons had the courage of a Hodding Carter II, the publisher of the *Delta Democrat*, or a Henry Meyer, the editor of the *Starkville Daily News*, or a Florence Mars, a resident of Philadelphia, Mississippi, to speak out against the cruelty and the evildoings of the Klan.

By the mid-1970s, things were, on the surface, different in Mississippi. By 1982 the last Mississippi counties were ending segregated public schools. By 1992 the U.S. Supreme Court, in *United States v. Fordice*, labeled the Mississippi system of public higher education racially unconstitutional and called for action to end formal segregation in the state's colleges and universities. And in the mid-1990s the Mississippi attorney general brought murder charges against some Klansmen for their violent acts against other civil rights advocates that occurred thirty years earlier.

By no means has racism ended in Mississippi and elsewhere in America. But society has forced, through law and public policy, some changes in the behavior of men and women by finally condemning the brutal racial violence that was endemic to many sections of the United States in the 1950s and 1960s. *Murder in Mississippi* tries to capture the fears, the hatred, the irrational behavior of those who lived and worked in the Deep South at that time. It also tries to convey the courage of many who responded to these racist actions at a time when they were openly and brazenly displayed for the world to see. It is important for Americans in the twenty-first century to never forget this earlier epoch of our cultural and political history. This is the foundational reason for the telling of the story of Mickey Schwerner, James Chaney, and Andy Goodman.

CHAPTER I

Driving on Highway 19 to Philadelphia, Mississippi

This is a terrible town, the worst I've seen. There is a complete reign of terror here.

MARTIN LUTHER KING, JR., 1964

It is October 1976, and I have been in Mississippi since July, having moved down to Mississippi State University from the New York metropolitan area, where I had been on the political science faculty at Hofstra University since 1965. I began teaching political science at Rutgers University in the summer of 1964, the "Mississippi Freedom Summer." I started in June 1964, the month in which three civil rights workers — Mickey Schwerner, J. E. Chaney, and Andy Goodman — were murdered by Klansmen outside Philadelphia, Mississippi. A dozen years later I was living in Mississippi, and on a warm and very humid Friday evening in October, I was traveling from Starkville, Mississippi, to Philadelphia, Mississippi.

Although I was soon to become involved in a variety of civil rights activities in the Magnolia State, this ride to Philadelphia had nothing to do with civil rights or justice or anything of importance. Put simply, I was the referee of a crew of high school football officials, and the five of us were on our way to officiate a game between bitter rivals: Philadelphia versus Neshoba County. For the others in the car, long-time residents of the state, the trip was uneventful, and their talk focused on reviewing football rules and such. I was not listening to the chatter because I was about to travel a historic road, one that scared the living daylights out of me.

After leaving Starkville, we went south on Highway 25, a state highway, for about thirty-five miles through the sleepy town of Louisville, Mississippi. By this time, it was quite dark. There were no overhead lights on these two-lane roads; the white line dividing the roadway was so worn that it was invisible most of the time. The only illumination was provided by the car's headlights. It was another seventeen miles south on Highway 25 before I spotted the sign for Philadelphia:

"Philadelphia, 18 miles, Left on Highway 19." I made the turn. I was now on Highway 19, the road taken by the three young civil rights workers a dozen years earlier as they traveled to Meridian, Mississippi (in neighboring Lauderdale County). I remember tightly gripping the car's wheel, half in fear, half in remembrance. My body was one large goose bump, and the hair on the back of my neck and on my arms was standing upright.

A few miles before I reached Philadelphia, the car crossed Highway 21. Had I traveled on that road a few miles southwest of the city of Philadelphia, I would have come upon a gravel road where the three civil rights workers' bodies were buried under a fifteen-foot earthen dam in late July 1964. Had I, instead, turned northeast on Highway 21, after driving about thirteen miles I would have entered the Choctaw Indian Reservation and quickly come upon Bogue Chitto Swamp. It was at this spot in June 1964 that the FBI found the charred car the three civil rights workers were driving the day they were stopped for speeding on the very road I was traveling, Highway 19.

For the first time in my life, I was in Neshoba County, on the road to Philadelphia, Mississippi, which Martin Luther King Jr. called a "terrible town, the worst [he had] seen." I was traveling on that same highway, where at least eighteen Klansmen waylaid and murdered Schwerner, Chaney, and Goodman only a dozen years earlier. I was actually traveling on the road to Philadelphia, the county seat of Neshoba County, and it was, and remains, the eeriest, scariest moment of my life.

Neshoba County, 570 square miles in area, is one of the smallest of Mississippi's eighty-two counties. It was created in 1833, as a result of the Treaty of Dancing Rabbit Creek. "Neshoba" is the Choctaw word for "wolf." In 1964, there were around 20,000 residents in the county, and Philadelphia's population was a little more than 4,000 persons. It was the only large town in Neshoba County, and all the lawyers living in the county, a total of five, practiced and lived there. (All of them would soon be retained as defense counsel for the men charged by the federal government with conspiring to murder Schwerner, Chaney, and Goodman.) There were about 14,000 whites in the county, with another 3,000 or so blacks and fewer than 3,000 Choctaw Indians. It was, like so many counties in Mississippi, dirt-poor, consisting of pastureland and piney woods, with the accompanying sawmills and terrible-smelling pulp mills. Most of the county residents were poor, with more than 25 percent of them living below the poverty level. More than half the population had less than a high school education. (In 2000, 21 percent of Neshoba County residents lived below the poverty level, the majority of them either children younger than eighteen or seniors over sixty-five years of age. And, in 2000, more than 65 percent of the population had graduated from high school.)

The state of Mississippi was, as Student Nonviolent Coordinating Committee (SNCC) leader Bob Moses said in 1961, the very "heart of the iceberg" of racism in America. W. J. Cash, in his classic portrayal of southern politics and culture, *The Mind of the South*, wrote of the state that it was "not quite a nation within a nation, but the next thing to it." In 1964, the Council of Federated Organizations (COFO) focused its Mississippi Freedom Summer project on that state because, in 1962, only 6.7 percent of Mississippi's blacks were registered to vote, the lowest percentage in the nation. And the county seat, Philadelphia, Mississippi, wrote David Nevin in *Life* magazine in 1964, "was a strange, tight little town where fear and hatred of things and ideas that come from the outside is nearly pathological."

Although blacks in the South had long been denied the right to vote by southern jurisdictions, even though the right to vote was guaranteed to all male citizens by the Fifteenth Amendment (ratified in 1870), there was no real effort to address that inequality until the 1930s and 1940s. Prior to the successful efforts by the National Association for the Advancement of Colored People (NAACP) to end the "white primary" in the South (*Smith v. Allwright*, 1944), there was little that advocates for the black community could do because of conservative U.S. Supreme Court decisions that went back to the 1870s. In great part the reason for the NAACP's acquiescence was because the U.S. Supreme Court, in 1896, handed down a major opinion, *Plessy v. Ferguson*. That opinion validated segregation of the races in all social situations, from birth to death, and defused almost all efforts to achieve racial equality, especially but not exclusively evident in the South.

When, in the *Brown* decision of 1954, the U.S. Supreme Court unanimously concluded that the 1896 *Plessy v. Ferguson* doctrine of "separate but equal" was no longer applicable in the field of public secondary education, the South exploded in wrathful anger. May 17, 1954, "decision Monday" for the Court during that era, instantly became known as "Black Monday" by many southerners. For the very first time in the history of racial relations in the South, an opinion of the U.S. Supreme Court struck at the very heart of the southern way of life: segregation, the absolute separation of the races.

The response in the Deep South, which included Mississippi, Alabama, Georgia, Florida, Louisiana, Texas, and South Carolina, was swift and multifaceted. Massive resistance, from these states' congressional representatives, state legislatures, and governors, from private citizens, from state judges and many federal district judges, was immediate and pervasive. For example, southern noncompliance with *Brown* was so extensive in this region that it was not until 1970, sixteen years after the watershed 1954 *Brown* decision, that Neshoba County finally began to integrate its public schools. (It would take another fifteen years until Mississippi's last holdout counties, in the southeastern part of the state, under court orders, reluctantly began to integrate their public schools — three decades after *Brown*.)

Beyond questionable legal and political "states' rights" arguments and strategies, other more financially threatening, violent, and more painful actions were taken to evade, avoid, and delay desegregation action in the Deep South. On July 11, 1954, less than two months after *Brown*, thirteen upscale Mississippi citizens met in Indianola, Mississippi, to create the Citizens Council. Within a year, chapters had been formed across the Deep South. Critics of the segregationists called these organizations "White Citizens Councils," a name that quickly caught on (and will be used in this book). A White Citizens Council chapter was organized in Neshoba County in late 1954 by two of the county's leading citizens. Florence Mars, a lifelong resident of Philadelphia and a vocal supporter of the civil rights movement in the 1960s, recalled in her memoir, *Witness in Philadelphia*, that "virtually everyone who was asked to, joined. Refusal would have been seen as an act of traitorous disloyalty to Mississippi and the South."

Fear of the WCC and the KKK was not the sole possession of the black community in the South in the years after the *Brown* decisions. Most whites living in the South at that time, as Mars suggests, were nearly as frightened of these virulent segregationist groups as were the blacks. And so the white majority became, a decade before Vice President Spiro Agnew coined the phrase, the "silent majority."

The White Citizens Council, labeled by outspoken liberal Mississippi newspaper publisher Hodding Carter Jr. the "uptown KKK," was formed in the months immediately following the May 1954 *Brown* decision. Its membership roster included the white, powerful, middle- and upper-class social elites in the town or city: wealthy businessmen, bankers, professors, doctors, lawyers, clergy (including a number of rabbis in Mississippi), and politicians — including Mississippi's former governor Ross Barnett. During the council's heyday in Mississippi, 1954–1965, observed Donna Ladd, it had more than 250,000 mem- bers — with connections in every level of Mississippi government.

Much more ominously, however, was the third reincarnation, in February 1964, of the Klan in Mississippi, the White Knights of the Mississippi Ku Klux Klan. The initial period of open Klan activity in America came at the close of the Civil War and ended a generation later. The second era of Klan activity in Mississippi and across the nation followed the end of World War I. During the 1920s the KKK was an extremely influential group in the electoral politics of the South. Many southern governors and U.S. senators (including Ala- bama's Senator Hugo L. Black, 1926–1937) owed their victories to open Klan support of their candidacies.

The Neshoba County Klavern was described, in 1964, by Inspec- tor Joseph Sullivan of the FBI, as "one of the strongest Klan units ever gathered [in the state] and one of the best disciplined groups." In 1964, there were only two paid Neshoba County law enforcement officers: forty-one-year-old, six-foot-two, 250-pound Sheriff Lawrence Rainey, who was elected in 1963. Deputy Sheriff Cecil Price was only a bit smaller, a lot younger (twenty-six years of age, a former Philadel- phia fireman), and not as gregarious as Rainey. Both were early join- ers of the Mississippi KKK and worked closely with the Neshoba County KKKers. Both attended meetings of the Neshoba Klavern and quite evidently supported the goals of the organization.

Rainey was born and raised in Neshoba County. He attended pub- lic school through the eighth grade and then quit to work as a mechanic before entering law enforcement. Before his 1963 election victory, Rainey served for four years as a policeman on the Philadelphia, Mis- sissippi, police force. During that time he shot and killed two African Americans "in the line of duty." Indeed, Rainey was elected in 1963 be- cause he was clearly seen as "hard on Negroes." After his election, a res- ident of Philadelphia, Mississippi, recalled:

Rainey swaggered around in Old West police get-up, complete with pointy boots, a menacing cowboy hat over his balding head, a six-shooter, a blackjack and a nightstick. He would spit his Red Man juice out of the window of the mammoth blue-gray Oldsmobile he drove around the town, shouting greetings to his friends and scowling at anyone, especially blacks, who got in his way.

Cecil Price had been a dairy supplies salesman and then the Philadelphia fire chief before his stint as deputy sheriff of Neshoba County. He had a reputation for terrorizing blacks in the county, and he was equally involved in beatings and brutality against blacks during his time in law enforcement. Given this raw reality of "law enforcement" in Neshoba County, blacks had no way to seek relief from the police brutality they were receiving from Rainey and Price.

For Sheriff Rainey and his fellow residents of Philadelphia and Neshoba County, there were two separate and unequal worlds: their white world and the "nigger" world. Rainey's task was to maintain the absolute — and unequal — separation of the two races. If outsiders, referred to by Rainey and his friends as "Commies" or "Jews" or "nigger lovers," invaded Mississippi to challenge the state's racist folkways, then Rainey's second task was to make sure they would not be comfortable while in the state and that they would be encouraged to quickly leave Mississippi.

On April 4, 1964, the *Neshoba Democrat*'s lead editorial, reflecting this view, was directed to Congress of Racial Equality (CORE) staffers such as Schwerner living and working in Lauderdale and Neshoba Counties, as well as to the hundreds of civil rights volunteers who, under the guidance and direction of COFO, were getting ready to come into the state in the summer of 1964. (COFO was the umbrella organization, created in 1963, for the three civil rights groups pledged to support the 1964 Mississippi Freedom Summer project: the NAACP, CORE, and SNCC.) The piece was written by the editor of the *Democrat*, Jack Long Tannehill, a relative of Louisiana's governor Huey P. Long, and himself a member of the White Citizens Council and one of the town's most outspoken segregationists: "All races here enjoy the very best of relationships, and many of us count our Negro citizens as true and loyal friends. We hope our status quo remains, and feel that others do, too, regardless of race. Outsiders who come in here and try to stir up trouble should be dealt with in a manner they won't forget."

An NAACP branch was established in Philadelphia in the late 1950s. It was, however, a very small and quiet group of African Americans and did not have a visible presence in the city. A turning point in Neshoba County African American political activity came after CORE established a headquarters in Meridian, Mississippi (in Lauderdale County, about forty miles southeast of Philadelphia on Highway 19), in 1963. Mickey Schwerner and his wife, Rita, were the first paid leaders assigned (on Thanksgiving Day, 1963) to the Meridian CORE center by the organization's leadership in New York City. They arrived in their VW van in late January 1964 to begin their civil rights work on February 1, 1964. One immediate task was to establish voting classes to prepare African Americans to register to vote. Another was to lay the groundwork for the Mississippi Freedom Summer project and the associated "Freedom School" activities for the dozens of volunteers who would be coming down to Lauderdale and Neshoba Counties during the upcoming summer of 1964.

The violent clash of unequal armies took place in the first half of 1964. On June 21, 1964, the three civil rights workers were brutally murdered by almost two dozen Klansmen in the dark of night off Highway 19, a few miles south of the town of Philadelphia. As a consequence, for the next three years a number of actions were taken by the federal government (the Department of Justice [DOJ] and the Federal Bureau of Investigation [FBI]), the Mississippi state government, the White Knights of the Mississippi KKK, and the secretive Mississippi State Sovereignty Commission (MSSC) investigators, as well as civil rights organizations, including the NAACP, SNCC, Southern Christian Leadership Conference (SCLC), and CORE.

Between December 1964 and October 1967, the following events took place:

- Indictments were filed in federal district court in Mississippi.
- The indictments were thrown out by a federal magistrate and a federal district court judge (both sitting in and ruling from the federal courthouse in Meridian, Mississippi).

- The DOJ took an appeal to the U.S. Supreme Court, 1965, and, in 1966, the justices unanimously overturned the dismissal of the indictments.
- In October 1967, eighteen Klansmen were finally brought into federal court to face conspiracy — not murder — charges. (The State of Mississippi has never brought these Klansmen into a state court to face murder charges.)
- Seven Klansmen were convicted of conspiracy and, in 1970, after they had exhausted their legal remedies, went off to federal penitentiaries.

A decade later, all had been released, and all returned to Philadelphia and Neshoba County to continue on with their lives. One of them, former deputy sheriff Cecil Price, became a watch repair craftsman in the City Jewelry establishment on the main square in Philadelphia in the mid-1970s. In the early 1990s he would be elected vice president of the Neshoba County Shriners.

Murder in Mississippi examines all these pieces of the tragedy that took place after 11:00 P.M. on Highway 19 in Philadelphia, Mississippi, on June 21, 1964. It is a story that captures the almost Manichaean struggle between the forces of light and the forces of darkness that existed in America at that time in history.

The U.S. Supreme Court's decision in *U.S. v. Price, et al.* was an important, unanimous one. The ruling enabled federal prosecutors to use nineteenth-century civil rights statutes to prosecute criminals who had escaped punishment for criminal acts in southern states. After the Supreme Court's ruling, in 1967, for the very first time in Mississippi history, white men were convicted of conspiring to take the lives and liberties of American citizens — black and white civil rights workers.

The convictions in the *Price* trial, however, were unique — because of the mass publicity surrounding the disappearance and murder of the three men, two of whom were white. In the *Annual Report of the U.S. Attorney General* (1967), it was noted that the Civil Rights Division almost always lost in federal court. In that year "there were no convictions in 12 trials against police officers for violating Section 242." James P. Turner, a lawyer with the Civil Rights Division from the early 1960s to 1993, cynically noted, in 1999, the existence of "an informal competition among Civil Rights Division lawyers in which the winner was the one whose *acquitting* jury stayed out the longest [my emphasis]. (The scale was on the order of 30 to 60 minutes, not counting any mealtimes occurring right before a jury returned. It was widely held that jurors would delay returning a verdict until after lunch or dinner.)"

To place the *Price* opinion of the High Bench in perspective, one must be aware of the events that preceded *Price*, as well as the events that followed the Supreme Court's decision. This is the task of the storyteller, the author of this book. It is a grim chronicle, and it does not have a very happy ending. In many ways, the story is not yet over, for a small number of Klansmen have evaded justice for their part in the cold-blooded killing of the three civil rights workers in late June 1964, forty years ago.

CHAPTER 2

Genesis

Mississippi and the Struggle for
Racial Equality

*You don't understand the fear. There was a great fear, that deep fear we [blacks]
had to live with daily. That fear is still strongly among us. It's never gone away.*

REVEREND CLINT COLLIER, NESHOBA COUNTY, 1964

The year 1954 was a signal breakthrough one for blacks in their struggle for equality. While long-established civil rights organizations such
as the NAACP, created in 1909, had been battling in the courts for
equality for blacks, it was a difficult war with modest successes. A
prime reason for the continuing dilemma was the enduring vitality of
the *Plessy* doctrine.

In *Plessy v. Ferguson*, 1896, a 7:1 U.S. Supreme Court majority validated state legislation that socially segregated the races. The Court
stated that as long as the separated facilities were equal, the Constitution's Fourteenth Amendment Equal Protection Clause was not
offended by such state laws. After all, the Court said, the Tenth Amendment gives to the states the police power to protect the public's health,
safety, welfare, and well-being. And if the community believed that the
two races were fundamentally different morally and intellectually, then
legislators could pass laws to absolutely segregate these groups.

Plessy was the Court's imprimatur legitimating the separation of the
races — ultimately, separation covered all social situations from birth
to death. By the beginning of World War I, America's system of Jim
Crow (the term given to formal and informal segregation practices)
meant that from hospitals — and doctors, nurses, pharmacies — to
cemeteries, and all social matters between, there would be absolute
separation. In 1946, there existed more than 250 statutes in twenty-
two states either compelling or permitting racial segregation in
schools, colleges, libraries, trains, waiting rooms, buses, professional
baseball teams, streetcars, steamboats, ferries, circuses, theaters, pub-

lic halls, parks, playgrounds, beaches, racetracks, poolrooms, hospitals, mental institutions, prisons, poorhouses, orphanages, and homes for the aged. Six states prohibited prisoners of different races to be chained together; one state required separate telephone books; another prohibited interracial boxing.

Ironically, during the pre–World War II (1933–1940) propaganda blitzkrieg by Nazi Germany broadcast to the northern sections of the United States, the Nazis pointed out that unlike America, with its thousands of lynchings of black persons and "Jimcrow Justice," Germany "does not kill our Jews," and blacks were not treated with disrespect. They were not segregated from others while visiting Nazi Germany. At the same time, in other broadcasts beamed to the southern section of America, the Nazi propaganda machine claimed that President Franklin D. Roosevelt and especially his wife, Eleanor, were planning on ending segregation in America and giving all minorities, especially blacks, their full voting rights.

For the lawyers in the NAACP, a civil rights organization created a year after the Springfield, Illinois, race riot of 1908 (the city was Abraham Lincoln's birthplace), the *Plessy* precedent meant that all they could do in court was to argue that the colored public municipal facility was separated from the white facility, but it was not the equal of the white facility. Because it was absolutely the case that the separate black facilities were unequal — elementary and secondary schools, teacher salaries, hospitals, parks, colleges, professional schools, and so forth — all the NAACP lawyer had to do was present the data to the courts. Through 1954, especially after the NAACP's 1938 victory in *Missouri ex rel Gaines v. Canada*, therefore, the NAACP won cases in federal courts (based on their use of the hated *Plessy* precedent) using the legal argument that, in this instance, separate is not equal. However, *Plessy* was still the law of the land midway into the twentieth century.

By 1947, however, through the instigation of Thurgood Marshall, the ardent and passionate head of the small band of lawyers in the NAACP's Legal and Educational Defense Fund (LDF), the NAACP leadership announced a major policy change. Henceforth, that organization's legal branch would no longer argue in court using the *Plessy* precedent; instead, it would challenge the very constitutionality of the "separate but equal" concept. Their argument was a basic one. The *Plessy* doctrine ran afoul of the Fourteenth Amendment's Equal Protection Clause, namely, that no state shall "deny any person within its jurisdiction the equal protection of the laws."

This change caused great consternation in the black communities affected by the separate but equal doctrine, primarily those in the Deep South. The reason was simple: After generations of absolutely unequal treatment of blacks by white legislators and educators, the successful NAACP litigation efforts found these communities receiving *promises* of much more money for education, including more per capita funds per student for new books, new science labs, new buildings, and buses for their children to ride to and from school, as well as vastly improved salaries for black teachers and administrators.

The leaders of these black communities wanted, as Thurgood Marshall called it, "deluxe Jim Crow." He said, perhaps half in jest, that his biggest headache in implementing the new policy was brought on because of the anger and intransigence of the black communities to accept the fundamental change in the NAACP's legal direction. After 1947, hundreds of letters were sent by the LDF lawyers to branch presidents in the South, informing them that the NAACP no longer went into state and federal courts to argue the "separate but not equal" legal strategy.

Henceforth, the NAACP's LDF would frontally challenge the constitutionality of the *Plessy* "separate but equal" doctrine. By 1951, Marshall and his staff were in the final stage of their challenge to the constitutionality of *Plessy* itself—in the area of public secondary education. By 1951, in four states (South Carolina, Kansas, Virginia, and Delaware) and in the District of Columbia, state courts and a federal court had heard arguments by both parties regarding the validity of separate schools for black and white children. In all these cases, the judges ruled against the NAACP, citing *Plessy* as precedent.

The Racial Watershed: The *Brown* Decisions

Brown v. Board of Education of Topeka, Kansas was one of five cases heard by the U.S. Supreme Court during its 1953 term. Four state cases were consolidated and argued together before the Court. The fifth public school segregation case, involving segregation in the nation's capital, was heard separately because it was not a state case. The "segregation cases," as they were called, were argued twice before the U.S. Supreme Court. The first arguments were heard for almost a week in December 1952. Because the justices were so fractured on the issue of overturning *Plessy* — leaning toward retention of the controversial, and hated, precedent — after hearing the cases in the fall of 1952, reargument was scheduled for the 1953 term of the Court.

Between these two oral arguments, a major change took place in the Court's personnel. Chief Justice Fred Vinson, a former Democratic politician from Kentucky (and a supporter of the *Plessy* doctrine) died in September 1953, one month before the second scheduled oral arguments. (Justice Felix Frankfurter, one of the brethren who opposed Vinson on the issue, said to Alexander Bickel, his law clerk, soon after hearing of the chief's death: "This is the first indication I have ever had that there is a God.")

President Eisenhower then filled the "center seat" with Governor Earl Warren of California, a Republican politician who had served as state attorney general before becoming governor. Warren had never served as a judge until he became chief justice of the United States. He received the appointment because of a promise Eisenhower made to him at the Republican National Convention in 1952. In return for Warren's directing the California delegation to vote for Eisenhower, Eisenhower promised the Californian that the first vacancy on the High Bench would be filled by Warren. In December 1953 (the arguments in the segregation cases were postponed for two months so that Herbert Brownell, the new Eisenhower administration's attorney general, could prepare and present the government's brief on the question of segregated public schools to the Court), oral arguments were made before the new chief.

In the secret conference session after the second set of oral arguments, the chief justice began the discussion of the segregation cases heard earlier in the week. According to Justice William O. Douglas's notes, Warren said to his colleagues:

The separate but equal doctrine rests on a basic premise that the Negro race is inferior [to the white race]. That is the only way to sustain *Plessy*. The argument of Negro counsel proves that they are not inferior. We can't set up one group apart from the rest of us and say they are not entitled to [the] same treatment as all others.

The [Civil War amendments] were intended to make equal those who were once slaves. That view causes some trouble perhaps — but I do not know how segregation can be justified in this day and age. I recognize that the time element is important in the deep south. So we must act in a tolerant way.

By mid-May 1954, Earl Warren had persuaded the other eight justices to unanimously strike down *Plessy*. Warren wrote the comparatively short, seventeen-page, watershed opinion for the Court. It was a nonaccusatory statement that did not single out the South for criticism: "We come then to the question presented: Does segregation of children in public schools solely on the basis of race, even though the physical facilities and other 'tangible' factors may be equal, deprive the children of the minority group of equal educational opportunities? We believe that it does." Rather than condemn the South and other areas of the nation, Warren said:

> Whatever may have been the extent of psychological knowledge [about the lifelong detrimental effect] upon the colored children at the time of *Plessy v Ferguson*, modern social and psychological science has shown that segregation creates "a sense of inferiority" [that adversely] affects the motivation of the child to learn. We conclude that in the field of public education the doctrine of "separate but equal" has no place. Separate educational facilities are inherently unequal. Therefore, we hold that the plaintiffs and others similarly situated for whom the actions have been brought are, by reason of the segregation complained of, deprived of the equal protection of the laws guaranteed by the Fourteenth Amendment.

Brown I signaled the beginning of a declared war between the southern segregationists and the civil rights groups and the federal district court judges who were ordered by the Supreme Court, in *Brown II*, 1955, to oversee, "with all deliberate speed," the end of segregated public schools.

In late May 1954, Tom Brady's condemnation of the Court's decision, entitled *Black Monday*, was published by the White Citizens Council and became the bible for segregationists across the nation. Politicians across the South unleashed their venom at the federal government in general and the Supreme Court in particular. For example, George C. Wallace, the future governor of Alabama, said of the federal courts:

> They assert more power than claimed by King George III, more power than Hitler, Mussolini, or Khrushchev ever had. They assert the power to declare unconstitutional our very thoughts. To create for us a system of moral and ethical values. To outlaw and declare unconstitutional, illegal, and immoral the customs, traditions, and beliefs of the people, and furthermore they assert the authority to enforce their decrees in all these subjects upon the American people without their consent.

Although *Brown* technically invalidated *Plessy* only in regard to segregated public schools, within two years it was cited as precedent in more than five dozen short (usually one or two paragraphs), unsigned per curiam opinions handed down by the Supreme Court that invalidated *Plessy*'s doctrine in other public areas as well. Segregated public beaches and bathhouses, municipal golf courses, municipal buses, public parks, athletic contests, airport restaurants, courtroom seating, and municipal auditoriums were all invalidated by the Court because they violated the Fourteenth Amendment's Equal Protection Clause.

Massive Southern Resistance to the Idea of Racial Equality

Implementing the *Brown* order to desegregate public schools, however, proved to be long, arduous, and extremely frustrating for the NAACP lawyers and the black plaintiffs. Part of the southern resistance to *Brown* involved legal evasion, avoidance, and delay of all orders to develop "good faith" desegregation plans. The NAACP lawyers had asked the Court to issue a "desegregate *now*" order to the South in *Brown*, but the justices thought that request was not practicable or even possible. A decade after *Brown*, 98 percent of black schoolchildren in the eleven southern states were still attending segregated public schools. (Ironically, in the 1968 case of *Green v. New Kent County School District, Virginia*, the Court unanimously concluded that the time for "all deliberate speed" had ended. Segregated school systems, wrote Justice William Brennan for a unanimous Court, had to "integrate immediately.")

Within two months of the Court's 1954 *Brown I* decision, the upscale racist organization, the White Citizens Council, was launched in Indianola, Mississippi, in Sunflower County, the home of powerful U.S. Senator James Eastland. For Robert T. Patterson, its creator, it was the nonviolent alternative to the Klan: "If we fail, the temper of the community may produce something like the Klan." Within months, there were White Citizens Council chapters formed across the South. Their message was a simple one: If blacks insisted on their rights, bank credit would be denied, bank loans would be called in, mortgages would be foreclosed, black farm tenants would be evicted, black businessmen would suffer, and jobs would be lost, including domestic work in the homes of white southerners.

The Eisenhower administration regularly received information from the FBI about the activities of the White Citizens Councils. In February 1956, for example, a chapter held a rally at the Alabama State Coliseum, in Montgomery, at which was distributed a "Preview of the Declaration of Segregation," a document that was given to Eisenhower later that month. It stated, in part:

> When in the course of human events it becomes necessary to abolish the Negro race, proper methods should be used. Among these are guns, bows and arrows, sling shots, and knives. We hold these truths to be self-evident, that all whites are created equal with certain rights; among these are life, liberty and the pursuit of dead niggers. . . . If we don't stop [them], we will soon wake up and find Rev. King in the White House.

White resistance to the civil rights movement after *Brown* was relentless, and it was very successful. By 1960, the White Citizens Council membership stood at 85,000 persons, and the organization had chapters in sixty-five of Mississippi's eighty-two counties. For a decade, from its inception through the crisis in 1964, through legal and economic sanctions brought against Mississippi blacks and pro-integration whites, it was winning skirmish after skirmish. The WCC succeeded in preventing the desegregation of the public schools in Mississippi, as well as workplaces, public and private facilities, and neighborhoods. Through its scare tactics, it prevented any appreciable increase in black voter registration.

The White Citizens Council successes made it unnecessary to formally reorganize the Mississippi Klan until February 1964. While there were also murders, lynchings, bombings of black homes and churches, recorded instances of police brutality, and beatings of blacks by whites in this decade, these were largely individual excesses by out-of-control white segregationists. One example of such behavior was the murder of fourteen-year-old Emmett Till by two white businessmen in Money, Mississippi, in August 1955 because the black youngster (visiting relatives from his home in Chicago) allegedly whistled at the wife of one of the men. (The two men were found not guilty of Till's murder by an all-white jury, which took a half hour to reach its verdict.) The Papers of the NAACP, especially Part 20, entitled "White Resistance and Reprisals, 1956–1965," found in the Library of Congress, thoroughly document these endless attacks on NAACP leaders such as Medgar Evers, as well as on ordinary black citizens trying to register to vote.

When the U.S. Supreme Court handed down its implementation order in *Brown II* in May 1955, calling for public school desegregation "with all deliberate speed," the war began in earnest. By the following March, political and economic resistance to federal court management of desegregation was fully mobilized. The Southern Manifesto, the "Declaration of Constitutional Principles," was introduced into the *Congressional Record* on March 12, 1956. It carried the signatures of nineteen U.S. senators and seventy-seven House members from the eleven southern states and expressed a determination to resist by any means necessary the Court's *Brown* decision of 1954. In part it stated:

> We regard the decision of the Supreme Court in the school cases as a clear abuse of judicial power. . . . This unwarranted exercise of power by the Court, contrary to the Constitution, is creating chaos and confusion in the States principally affected. It is destroying the amicable relations between the white and Negro races that have been created through 90 years of patient effort by the good people of both races. . . . Without regard to the consent of the governed, outside agitators are threatening immediate and revolutionary

changes in our public-school systems. . . . We pledge ourselves to use all lawful means to bring about a reversal of this decision which is contrary to the Constitution and to prevent the use of force in its implementation.

President Eisenhower, at a press conference immediately after the manifesto was issued, was asked to comment on that development as well as other massive resistance actions of the South. His response, on March 14, 1956, reflected his own conservative views about the general issue of integration of the races and his great sympathy for the people in the South after *Brown* was announced:

> Now, the first thing about the manifesto is this: that they say they are going to use every legal means. No one in any responsible position anywhere has talked nullification because — and there would be a place where we get to a very bad spot for the simple reason I am sworn to defend and uphold the Constitution and, of course, I can never abandon or refuse to carry out my duty. . . . We are not talking here about coercing, using force. . . . Now let us remember this one thing, and it is very important: The people who have this deep emotional reaction on the other side were not acting over the past three generations in defiance of law. They were acting in compliance with the law as interpreted by the Supreme Court of the United States under the decision of 1896 [*Plessy*].

By 1956, the White Citizens Council was near its apex as an anti-desegregation organization across the South. In April 1956, a national organization, the Citizens Councils of America, was established in New Orleans, Louisiana. By the end of 1956, it was functioning in the eleven southern states and had a membership of 300,000.

About the same time, on March 29, 1956, the Mississippi State Sovereignty Commission was established "for the maintenance of racial segregation." Its creation was also a direct consequence of the Court's *Brown* decisions. In the gubernatorial race in Mississippi in the fall of 1955, the winner was the man who "outsegregated" his opponents: James P. Coleman, who during the campaign pledged to create "a permanent authority for the maintenance of racial segregation with a full staff and funds for its operation to come out of tax money."

In the legislation creating the Sovereignty Commission, its duties and responsibilities were laid out in Section 5:

It shall be the duty of the commission to do and perform any and all acts and things deemed necessary and proper to protect the sovereignty of the State of Mississippi, and her sister States, from encroachment thereon by the Federal Government . . . and to resist the usurpation of the rights and powers reserved to this State and our sister States by the Federal Government on any branch, department, or agency thereof.

From 1956 until its official close in 1977 (its funding had been vetoed in 1973 by Governor Bill Waller), the Sovereignty Commission was the secretive "keeper of the State's rigid racial conformity." At the time of its closure, it had spied on more than 87,000 persons its investigators suspected of planning "subversive" acts against the people and traditions of Mississippi. Its essential purposes were to preserve the rigidly enforced Jim Crow system of segregation in the state and, unofficially working with the White Citizens Council, to oppose school desegregation in Mississippi.

The Sovereignty Commission quickly became the model for other state agencies; for example, that same year the Louisiana State Sovereignty Commission, the Alabama State Sovereignty Commission, the Florida Constitutional Commission, and the Virginia Commission on Constitutional Government were founded by state legislators. The Mississippi organization had twelve appointed members, including state legislators and gubernatorial appointees. The governor, lieutenant governor, state House speaker, and attorney general were ex officio members. An executive director was immediately hired to run the organization, which initially consisted of two departments: public relations and investigation. The former office was given a budget to enable the director to prepare publicity that positively presented the state to the nation. The first investigators hired were a former chief of the Mississippi Highway Patrol and a former FBI agent. The first budget, in 1956, was $250,000.

From its beginning, the most secretive part of the Sovereignty Commission was its investigation department. The department hired investigators, who in turn hired informants, including black informants, to spy on civil rights groups and individuals who were identified as civil rights supporters, including such personalities as Harry Belafonte, Joan Baez, and even Mississippi's own Elvis Presley. Other secret files were opened for individuals and associations such as Angela Davis, the Black Panthers, the Ford Foundation, UNICEF, James Baldwin, James Meredith, Jesse Jackson, Martin Luther King Jr., and Charles and Medgar Evers.

Many blacks living in the state had objected to the NAACP's 1947 policy change, and a few of them became informants for the Sovereignty Commission. Men such as the Reverend H. H. Humes; Fred Miller, an educational administrator; B. L. Bell, the principal of the all-black H. M. Nailor Elementary School in Cleveland, Mississippi; W. A. Higgins, superintendent of the Clarksdale, Mississippi, black public schools; H. McLaurin, president of Cohahoma Junior College; and O. M. McNair, the principal of the all-black high school in Belzoni, Mississippi, provided information about the goings-on in the civil rights movement in their state.

Time and again, when reviewing the once-secret files of the Sovereignty Commission, one sees these informant reports describing COFO and CORE activities from the inside out. For example, one report from "Operator F," a black informant, dated August 10, 1964, to the Sovereignty Commission, gave detailed information about the personnel in the COFO headquarters and the whereabouts of COFO's leaders:

> Mary King a white girl works at this office. . . . There is another girl who works at COFO by the name of "Casey" [Hayden]. . . . It was learned that Mendy Samstein is now working out of the McComb COFO office. He is a w/m . . . from New York. He is personally known to informant. Robert Moses [the director of COFO] left Hdqs Sunday morning for Meridian. . . . Investigation will continue.

In addition to the secret informants, the Sovereignty Commission had a number of paid investigators whose task was to gather information about civil rights actions, as well as responses to civil rights activities by segregationists in the state. A week before the three civil rights workers were murdered in late June 1964, the Sovereignty Commission sent one of its investigators into Neshoba County to look into the beatings of the black deacons of the burned-down Mount Zion Methodist Church. Sheriffs Rainey and Price told the investigator that they did not investigate the church bombing because no one had officially reported the event to them. The Sovereignty Commission investigator wrote that the blacks had not reported the incident to Rainey "because they considered him a suspect in the beatings."

Further, the commission was involved in the creation of "misinformation" about civil rights leaders. This manufactured information was then spread by the organization's public relations department. Immediately, as seen in the commission's correspondence, a symbiotic relationship developed between the governmental agency and the private group, the White Citizens Council. From 1960 to 1964 the Sovereignty Commission gave more than $190,000 in state funds to the White Citizens Council.

Civil Rights Organizational Activity in Mississippi

The NAACP was the primary civil rights organization fighting for racial equality from its inception in 1909 through the middle of the 1950s. By the time Thurgood Marshall stepped away from the leadership of the LDF in 1961 (when he was appointed to the U.S. Court of Appeals, Second Circuit, by President John F. Kennedy, as part of the "deal" that saw Harold Cox, who was a central figure in the *Price* trial, appointed to the U.S. District Court, Southern District, Mississippi), the organization had achieved legal victories in thirty-nine of forty-five cases argued before the U.S. Supreme Court since the third decade of the twentieth century.

By the middle of the century, the NAACP had branches in every state of the Union and more than 1 million members. Its key strategies for achieving racial equality were two: lobbying political leaders for changes in policy, and litigating in state and federal courts for equal rights. Unlike newer civil rights organizations that would emerge in the 1940s and 1950s, the NAACP rarely called for a marshaling of its members in order to try to change public policy through nonviolent direct action (marches, sit-ins, freedom rides, etc).

The NAACP held quite a contrary view of direct action. Thurgood Marshall, one among many of the organization's leaders, was always critical of these nonviolent direct actions. In 1947, he said that the "civil disobedience movement on the part of Negroes and their white allies, if employed in the South, would result in wholesale slaughter with no good achieved."

He vigorously objected to the Montgomery Improvement Association (MIA) boycott led by a young minister, Martin Luther King Jr., of the Montgomery, Alabama, bus system, fearing that such black actions would trigger outbursts of violence by Klansmen and other segregationists. When the U.S. Supreme Court ruled in 1956 that the city's segregated bus system had to end, Marshall told King that the legal actions taken by the NAACP in the lower courts and before the U.S. Supreme Court, not nonviolent direct action, ended segregation in Montgomery. "It was inappropriate to jeopardize the lives of youngsters when the goal could be achieved through litigation in the courts," he said at the time.

The NAACP's policy of not confronting opponents on the streets did not, however, stop the White Citizens Council from creating and then maintaining a hostile, anarchic atmosphere in the state, one that led violent individuals to commit murder. In 1961, Herbert Lee, an NAACP leader in McComb, Mississippi, was shot dead on the street outside McComb's city hall by E. W. Hurst, a Mississippi legislator. Lee was on his way to assist other blacks in registering to vote when Hurst killed him. The coroner's jury concluded that the murder was justified — self-defense was its judgment. Louis Allen, who witnessed the killing but was refused protection by the FBI, was found dead on January 31, 1964.

Another civil rights organization was founded in 1942 by college students in Chicago: the Congress of Racial Equality. Early members of CORE included George Hauser, James Farmer, Anna Murray, and Bayard Rustin. They were pacifists, and many became conscientious objectors and refused to serve in the military during World War II. They were greatly influenced by the writings of American philosopher Henry David Thoreau and the teachings of Mohandas Gandhi, who waged a successful nonviolent civil disobedience campaign against the British in India after World War I. These young CORE members believed that Gandhi's ideas and strategies could be used to nonviolently end racial discrimination in America.

One of CORE's first tactical actions, in early 1947, was labeled by

{ *Murder in Mississippi* }

the organization the "Journey of Reconciliation." The plan, created by Hauser and Rustin, called for eight whites and eight blacks to ride interstate buses for a two-week period — through Virginia, North Carolina, Tennessee, and Kentucky — to test the U.S. Supreme Court's ruling in *Morgan v. Virginia*, 1946, which called for desegregation of all interstate travel. In North Carolina, some members of the group were arrested for violating that state's Jim Crow bus statute and were sentenced to thirty days on a prison chain gang. The local judge, Henry Whitfield, excoriated the white members of this group of bus riders: "It's about time you Jews from New York learned that you can't come down here bringing your niggers with you to upset the customs of the South. Just to teach you a lesson, I gave your black boys 30 days, and I give you 90."

For the next two decades, CORE continued to plan and implement other nonviolent direct actions aimed at publicizing the reality of racial discrimination. By 1961, it had fifty-three chapters throughout the United States. James Farmer was the national director of the organization, and he worked with SNCC to organize student sit-ins during 1961. Within the year (three years before the passage of the 1964 Civil Rights Act) these sit-ins ended restaurant and lunch counter segregation in twenty-six southern cities. In 1963, a younger, fierier leader, Floyd McKissick, replaced Farmer.

That year was to be the beginning of the heightened tensions between the civil rights workers and the segregationists that would explode during the violent summer of 1964. In August 1963, CORE was instrumental in organizing the watershed March on Washington. More than 200,000 people of all races marched peacefully to the Lincoln Memorial to demand equal justice for all people in America. At the end of the all-day rally, Martin Luther King Jr. gave his famous and moving "I Have a Dream" speech.

In December 1955, another civil rights group saw the light of day in Montgomery, Alabama. Rosa Parks, a black resident of the city and one of the officers of the local branch of the NAACP, refused to take a seat in the back of a public bus and was arrested for violating the local Jim Crow ordinance. Within a week, the boycott of Montgomery's buses by the black community led to the creation of the MIA. A young Baptist preacher, Martin Luther King Jr., was selected to lead the group. The boycott lasted for more than a year until, in

November 1956, the U.S. Supreme Court, *in Gayle v. Browder*, ruled that separating passengers by race on municipal transportation violated the Fourteenth Amendment's Equal Protection Clause.

The following year, the MIA transmogrified into the Southern Christian Leadership Conference (SCLC), with Reverend King as its leader. Central to its direct-action strategy was the coordination of African American organizations, especially black churches, in the effort to overturn segregation and racial discrimination in voting.

A major technique of the SCLC was the marshaling of thousands of young blacks, from secondary school age to college age, to picket against these evils. Using these masses to stage lengthy peaceful protests in southern cities and towns — Birmingham, Alabama, and Albany, Georgia — the SCLC was able to publicize the presence of racial segregation, to demand an end to its practice, and to show the nation how these southern segregationists treated blacks who were peacefully protesting.

In April 1960, the SCLC saw many college-age men and women establish the sit-in movement to protest racial discrimination in private and public places open to members of the public. Within months, yet another civil rights organization was created: the Student Nonviolent Coordinating Committee. Like the SCLC, its parent organization, the SNCC was committed to peaceful, nonviolent direct actions that addressed voting discrimination in the Deep South, especially in those states that had not been the targets of SCLC actions, particularly Mississippi, the "middle of the iceberg" of racism. The SNCC's statement of purpose, published in August 1961, emphasized these values:

> We affirm the philosophical or religious ideal of nonviolence as the foundation of our purpose, the presupposition of our faith, and the manner of our action. Nonviolence as it grows from Judaic-Christian tradition seeks a social order of justice permeated by love. . . . Through nonviolence, courage displaces fear; love transforms hate. Acceptance dissipates prejudice; hope ends despair. Peace dominates war. Faith reconciles doubt. Mutual regard cancels enmity. Justice for all overthrows injustice.

In May 1961, a reenergized CORE organization implemented a strategy it labeled "Freedom Rides." This was an effort to integrate interstate public buses and the bus terminals servicing these vehicles in the South by having small groups of black and white CORE members ride interstate buses together and then to attempt, peacefully, to integrate the segregated bus terminals in Anniston, Birmingham, and Montgomery, Alabama, and Jackson, Mississippi.

The departure point for the Freedom Rides was Washington, D.C. Before the CORE activists boarded a bus, James Farmer, the organization's director, wrote letters to President Kennedy, the U.S. attorney general, the director of the FBI, the chairman of the Interstate Commerce Commission, and the Greyhound and Trailways companies, informing all of them about the project and presenting them with the itinerary. By posting the letters, Farmer "hoped that there would be protection. Indeed, that was one of the reasons we sent a letter to the FBI. We had thought that the FBI would provide protection for us, would see to it at each stop that we were not brutalized or killed." However, there was no federal protection — and there certainly was no police protection in these southern stops — for the integrated CORE group. When the Greyhound pulled into the Anniston, Alabama, bus terminal, rabid segregationists armed with bats and rocks greeted them, and the civil rights group told the driver to get back on the interstate. By the time the bus left, its tires had been slashed, and all the tires blew out on the highway. Farmer, on board the bus, later commented:

> Members of the mob had boarded cars and followed the bus, and now with the disabled bus standing there, the members of the mob surrounded it, held the door closed, and a member of the mob threw a firebomb into the bus, breaking a window to do so. Incidentally, there were some local policemen mingling with the mob, fraternizing with them while this was going on.

The occupants were able to escape through the rear of the bus, but just barely. The FBI had informed the local police departments of the CORE itinerary, but the FBI also knew that some of the police were Klansmen. In Montgomery, Alabama, the mob dragged CORE workers out of the bus and nearly killed a number of the white CORE volunteers with blows to the head.

U.S. Attorney General Robert Kennedy ordered 600 U.S. Marshals into Maxwell Air Force Base outside Montgomery to protect the CORE riders and the hundreds of other civil rights activists who flew into the state capital to support the besieged bus riders. The CORE contingent finally reached the Mississippi state line. When the buses crossed the line, they were greeted with an unusual sight: hundreds of Mississippi National Guardsmen "flanking the highway with their guns pointed toward the forest on both sides of the road." Evidently there were rumors of a bloody ambush by Klansmen, and the governor had called out the Guard. The ambush did not materialize, however, and the buses rolled into the Jackson, Mississippi, bus terminal.

Another surprise was waiting there: the only people in the terminal were state police, who arrested the CORE passengers for trespass as they stepped off the buses. The next day they were all convicted and sentenced to sixty days in the state maximum security prison at Parchman. Clearly, this event showed the virulent hostility of the South toward these outside agitators. It also pointed out the casualness with which the new Kennedy administration treated the possibility of violence to the bus riders. It was a painful learning process.

Beginning in 1961, the SNCC initiated voter registration drives in the heart of Dixie: Mississippi and Alabama. In July 1961, the first voter registration project began in McComb, Mississippi, under the direction of Robert Moses, a twenty-six-year-old, Harlem-born black schoolteacher who left teaching in 1960 to work as the SNCC's field secretary in Mississippi. SNCC workers joined with CORE to implement this and other voter registration activities in Mississippi.

This cooperation led, in 1962, to the creation of the COFO, an organization that continued the cooperative efforts of CORE and SNCC workers but also included the Mississippi NAACP leadership. The NAACP's state leader, Aaron Henry, became the president of COFO; Bob Moses was selected as activities codirector along with Dave Dennis, the field secretary in Mississippi for CORE.

In September 1962, the federal courts ordered the University of Mississippi (Ole Miss) to allow James Meredith, a twenty-nine-year-old black air force veteran, to enroll. He was accompanied to the university by John Doar of the U.S. Department of Justice and U.S. Marshal John McShane.

When word of Meredith's arrival went out, segregationists by the hundreds began to pour onto the campus in protest. President Kennedy, like his predecessor, President Dwight D. Eisenhower, in Little Rock, Arkansas, in September 1957, was forced to use federal marshals and troops from the 82nd and 101st Airborne — in the end, more than 25,000 troops — to quell the rioting that broke out that night. Guns were fired. Bottles and bricks were thrown at the troops and federal marshals and at Baxter Hall, which housed Meredith. Military trucks were turned over and set ablaze. Twenty-eight marshals were hit by bullets. Two civilians, one a foreign journalist covering the event, were killed by gunfire.

The following morning, October 1, 1962, Meredith prepared to enroll at Ole Miss. The rioting continued. Tear gas and the sounds of gunshots filled the morning air. The leader of the rioters, retired U.S. Army Major General Edwin A. Walker, forced out of the military because of his extremely conservative views, encouraged segregationists from across the South to join in this fight against integration: "Bring your flags, your tents, and your skillets." However, after another day of rioting, the regular Army airborne troops ended it. Meredith entered the university, but Airborne troops accompanied him everywhere because of the real fear that he would be injured or killed.

By 1963, the NAACP, CORE, and SNCC leaders began to focus on the state of Mississippi, which heretofore had been shunned by civil rights activists. As one SNCC worker said, "If we can crack Mississippi, we can crack segregation anywhere." The SCLC was continuing its nonviolent direct actions in Alabama and Georgia. The NAACP's hard-pressed LDF lawyers were thoroughly involved in the minutiae of school desegregation litigation, handling hundreds of school desegregation cases in 1963.

In April 1963, around Easter time, King and hundreds of his SCLC followers were marching in Birmingham, Alabama, in an effort to bring integration to that major southern city. Hundreds were arrested for violating a local court's temporary restraining order prohibiting them from marching on Easter Sunday. In 1967, a closely divided U.S. Supreme Court, splitting 5:4 on the merits in the case of *Walker v. Birmingham*, upheld the convictions.

On June 11, 1963, in another watershed event, President Kennedy went on national television to call for the passage of a comprehensive civil rights bill that would end racial discrimination in society, whether it was practiced by private or state actors. After lengthy delays and filibusters by southern representatives and senators — tabbed "bitter-enders" by their opponents and the media — the Civil Rights Act was signed into law on July 2, 1964, by President Lyndon Baines Johnson.

That June evening, after listening to Kennedy's speech, Medgar Evers, the NAACP's Mississippi field secretary, drove to his home in Jackson. Waiting for him in the bushes across the street was a lone gunman, Byron de la Beckwith, who murdered the civil rights leader. De la Beckwith, a fertilizer salesman and a member of the Greenwood, Mississippi, White Citizens Chapter, was charged with murder; he was freed, however, because two different juries deadlocked on a verdict, and mistrials were declared. In the 1970s, de la Beckwith ran for lieutenant governor in the Democratic Party primary but lost. Finally, in 1994, he was again charged with murdering Evers; this time a Mississippi state jury found him guilty, and he was sentenced to life imprisonment.

In September 1963, four young black girls — Cynthia Wesley, Carol Robertson, Addie Mae Collins, all fourteen years of age, and Denise McNair, eleven years old — were murdered while attending Sunday school classes in the Sixteenth Street Baptist Church, in Birmingham, Alabama. (More than thirty years later, one of the murderers, Thomas Blanton Jr., a Klansman, was finally tried and convicted for the deaths. By 2000, three other Klansmen were tried and convicted for their participation in the bombing of the church and the murders of the four girls.)

Reacting to the Birmingham church tragedy, Mickey Schwerner, then a social worker in New York City and a member of CORE, made the fateful decision to apply to CORE's national office in the city for a posting somewhere in the South. His wife, Rita, would join him in this request. In his application, Mickey wrote:

> As a social worker I have dedicated my life to social ills. However, my profession as yet has not become directly involved in the most devastating social disease at the present time — discrimination. I also feel that the Negro in the South has an even more bitter fight ahead of him than in the North and I wish to be part of that fight. In essence I would feel guilty and almost hypocritical if I do not give full time for an extended period.

In her application, Rita Schwerner, a New York City public school teacher in South Jamaica, Queens, wrote:

Since I have become active in CORE here in New York, I have become increasingly aware of the problems which exist in the Southern states. . . . I wish to become an active participant rather than a passive onlooker. As my husband and I are in close agreement as to our philosophy and involvement in the civil rights struggle, I wish to work near him, under the direction of CORE, in whatever capacity I may be most useful. My hope is to someday pass on to the children we may have a world containing more respect for the dignity and worth of all men than that world which was willed to us.

The couple was hired as CORE staffers on Thanksgiving Day in 1963 and was assigned to the Meridian, Mississippi, field office. They moved to that state in mid-January 1964. Less than six months later, Mickey Schwerner would be murdered along with his two fellow civil rights workers, James "J. E." Chaney and Andy Goodman.

In November 1963, COFO sponsored a "Freedom Vote: Campaign for Governor" project. Using more than 100 white college students as pollsters and voter advisers, most recruited from Yale and Stanford Universities, more than 80,000 blacks cast unofficial "freedom" ballots for governor and lieutenant governor. This very successful program led COFO to take the step that triggered Klan violence in 1964: planning for the Mississippi Freedom Summer project. The plan called for ten times the number of college students to spend the summer of 1964 in towns and cities across Mississippi to help black voters register to vote. In November 1963, however, FBI director J. Edgar Hoover spoke words that chilled the hearts of the civil rights leaders in Mississippi. Hoover stated: "We don't guard anyone. We do not wet nurse those who go down to reform the South." The civil rights groups heard this ominous message more than once from other FBI leaders and from officials in the U.S. Department of Justice. The message was also heard by the men who were planning the return of the Mississippi KKK.

In December 1963, arch-segregationists, concerned and hopping mad about the past and projected activities of CORE in their state and seeing that the White Citizens Council's largely nonviolent efforts to curtail these assorted "hippies, beatniks, Jews, and Commies" did not deter the civil rights groups, made the fateful decision to reformulate the White Knights of the Mississippi Ku Klux Klan. The organization was reintroduced in the state in February 1964.

Thus, with the coming of the new year in 1964, the stage was set for Mississippi burning: many hundreds of Freedom Summer participants were to experience the venomous hatred of the Klan in the state's long, hot summer days and nights. By summer's end, the "body count" reflected the brutality of the Mississippi Klan: thirty-five shootings (six black civil rights workers were killed between January and May 1964 while planning the summer project); Schwerner, Chaney, and Goodman murdered in June; four others wounded; thirty black home bombings; thirty-seven churches burned; more than 1,000 Freedom Summer students arrested; at least eighty beatings of black and white civil rights workers, by white mobs and racist police officers; and untold numbers of harassing and threatening telephone calls. (Rita Schwerner recalled, in a news story many years later, that at their tiny apartment in Meridian, the telephone rang all hours of the night with threats against her husband, Mickey, the callers saying over and over again, "That Jewboy is dead!") By summer's end, the Mississippi Klan had grown dramatically — from only 300 Klansmen in February to more than 6,000 in October 1964.

The Archenemies: The KKK versus the COFO

The revived Mississippi Klan was the violent counterforce to the efforts of COFO to change the political and social landscape of the state. For the Mississippi Klansmen, the "invasion" of the hated outsiders was upon the state, and only violence, bloodshed, and murder would quell the "civil righters."

The primary focus of their unmitigated anger was the trio of civil rights organizations that had the temerity to enter the Magnolia State and attempt to end a way of life that had existed for more than a century: the NAACP, CORE, and SNCC. The upcoming bloody, violent clash was a one-sided war because the civil rights groups were committed to nonviolence as a fundamental operating principle and because the federal government's policy was noninterference in this struggle between local communities and the civil rights forces bent on challenging the segregationist folkways. The war began in February 1964 and did not end until the following December, when eighteen Klansmen were charged with conspiring to take the lives of the three CORE workers, Schwerner, Chaney, and Goodman. Fundamentally, the battle was fought over deeply held and mutually exclusive sets of values about human existence, equality and inequality, and how society must be structured. However, it involved a very small segment of the Mississippi population — about 7,000 Klansmen — and a much smaller group of mostly outsiders, namely, the civil rights volunteers and the handful of professional civil rights workers. The vast majority of white Mississippians, while comfortable with the folkways of their state, by no means agreed with the violent tactics of the Klansmen. They were silent because they were frightened of the consequences of speaking out against the violence. They were bystanders to the mayhem foisted by their violent neighbors.

Epitomizing these basic differences between the Klan and the civil rights workers were four men: Sam Bowers, the newly selected Imperial Wizard of the White Knights of the Mississippi Ku Klux Klan; Edgar Ray "Preacher" Killen, the recruiting leader of the Lauderdale County and Neshoba County KKKs; Bob Moses, the director of the Mississippi Freedom Summer project of COFO; and Mickey Schwerner, the CORE leader in charge of the Meridian, Mississippi, office.

Sam Bowers

Samuel Holloway Bowers Jr., of Laurel, Mississippi, was thirty-nine years of age in February 1964 when he was selected as the Imperial Wizard of the White Knights of the Mississippi KKK. He was born in New Orleans in August 1924. His parents lived comfortably, and he was descended from a long line of politically active relatives. His grandfather, Eaton J. Bowers Sr., for example, served in the U.S. House of Representatives from 1903 until 1911.

In 1964, Sam Bowers was a partner in a jukebox and vending machine company, the Sambo Amusement Company. A navy veteran who had served in World War II, he attended college after mustering out of the service in 1945, including two years of study at Tulane University and the University of Southern California. He organized the Mississippi Klan and was elected its Imperial Wizard in February

1964. He served as leader for four years, until his conviction in 1967 for his role in the murders of the three CORE workers. For Bowers, the Klansmen were "Christian militants dedicated to oppose in every honorable way possible the forces of Satan on this earth."

In February 1966, Bowers and many of his Mississippi Klansmen were subpoenaed by the House Un-American Activities Committee (HUAC) to appear before the committee in Washington, D.C. HUAC was investigating the activities of the Klan in Mississippi and wanted to hear from the Imperial Wizard. Bowers "took" the Fifth Amendment protection against self-incrimination throughout the hearing, refusing to say whether documents and written orders attributed to him were actually his words. Committee investigators presented many documents that clearly reflected Bowers's religious beliefs and theories. For example, one document read to Bowers, allegedly written by him, exhorted Klansmen to "keep a Bible" with them at all times and to bear no ill will when eliminating enemies: "If it is necessary to eliminate someone, it should be done with no malice, in complete silence, and in the manner of a Christian act."

As in Klan organizations across the nation, secrecy was essential for the smooth functioning of the Mississippi KKK. Bowers created and implemented a secret code when ordering attacks on persons or structures: Number 1 was a cross burning; Number 2 was a whipping; Number 3 was a firebombing; and Number 4 was a killing. As a former Klansman and FBI informant told a jury in 1998, "Sam Bowers was the only man who could order a No. 3 and No. 4 in the KKK of the State of Mississippi."

Bowers considered himself the high priest, the "Warrior Priest," of white Christian militancy and viewed civil rights workers as the "betrayers of Jesus the Galilean." In an interview with Charles Marsh, a professor of religion at the University of Virginia, the only one he has given, Bowers maintained:

There are two really powerful figures in the world: the priest and the preacher. I think I came here as a priest, though not a preacher. A priest is interested in visible, public power operations; this is what makes him powerful as a warrior. A preacher is an evangelist; he will tell people what to do. But the priest will arrange the means and operations to implement this into concrete action. When the priest sees the heretic, he can only do one thing: he eliminates him.

The heretic cannot be forgiven; he must be eliminated. For Bowers, that meant getting rid of the civil rights activists, that is, the "liberal media whores," the "pagan academics," the Jews, Communists, homosexuals, atheists, and their sympathizers in order to save the white Christian nation. They were all, he wrote, "dedicated agents of Satan, absolutely determined to destroy Christian civilization and Christians." God had called Bowers to the urgent task of destroying these "heretics." He was committed to an aggressive and violent policy, one that attacked the forces of evil invading his beloved state. For Bowers, the Mississippi Freedom Summer participants were invading the state to "crucify the innocent people of God." And for the Imperial Wizard, the Klansmen were on a holy crusade to "murder these infidels."

Bowers's conspiracy theory was the core of his being and the basis for the Klan violence that continued until he was sent off to federal prison in Washington State in 1970. Bowers read and interpreted the Bible "with all the passion of a Fundamentalist Baptist." From his business in Laurel, a tiny town about sixty miles southwest of Meridian, he saw the CORE Jew, Mickey "Goatee" Schwerner, as a visible manifestation of the Antichrist, Satan (Schwerner had a goatee adorning his face when he arrived in Mississippi). And, in April 1964, he issued a Number 4 order to the Lauderdale-Neshoba Klavern: kill the activist CORE leader. It was one of at least nine such Number 4 orders Bowers issued from 1964 to 1967 as Imperial Wizard.

Another Number 4 order from Bowers led to the murder by fire of a black civil rights leader. At 2:00 A.M. on January 10, 1966, a carload of Klansmen threw gasoline bombs at the house of Vernon Dahmer Sr., a Hattiesburg, Mississippi, businessman and president of the Forrest County branch of the NAACP, who had been helping blacks register to vote. The house was engulfed in flames, but Dahmer managed to get his wife and daughter out through the rear of the building. Gunshots were fired into the house, and Dahmer returned fire.

Although he eventually escaped the inferno, he died thirteen hours later of severe burns about the head, face, arms, and upper body. Bowers and fourteen others were indicted and charged in state court with arson and the murder of Dahmer. Thirteen men came to trial, four were convicted, and one pleaded guilty. In addition, eleven of them were tried in federal court on charges of conspiring to take away Dahmer's protected constitutional rights. Bowers was not found guilty because of a mistrial and escaped justice. From 1966 through his fifth trial in 1998, Bowers maintained his innocence — as he did when charged with conspiracy to deprive Schwerner, Chaney, and Goodman of their rights protected by the Constitution.

Bowers's first four Dahmer trials ended in mistrials because the juries could not reach a unanimous verdict. On August 22, 1998, however, the fifth jury found Bowers guilty of ordering Dahmer's murder and sentenced him to life imprisonment. Bowers is presently serving his sentence in the Central Mississippi Correctional Facility in Rankin County.

In December, 2002, there appeared on the KKK Web site a "!!!FREE SAM BOWERS!!!" broadside. It called for the release of Bowers because two of his basic constitutional rights were violated: the Fourth Amendment protection against double jeopardy and the Sixth Amendment guarantee of the right to a speedy trial. The missive concluded: "Sam Bowers and his men stood courageously, at great personal sacrifice and without reward, to preserve Southern Heritage and rights. THERE IS NO DOUBT THAT SAM BOWERS IS THE GREATEST AND MOST HEROIC DEFENDER OF WHITE PEOPLE'S RIGHTS OF THIS ERA. HAIL SAM BOWERS!"

Edgar Ray "Preacher" Killen

One of Sam Bowers's most important men was Edgar Ray "Preacher" Killen, the Kleagle (recruiter and organizer) of the Lauderdale-Neshoba County Klavern whose house was Klan headquarters for Neshoba County. Preacher Killen is the great-great-great-great-great-grandson of Henry Killen, the son of an Irish immigrant who settled in South Carolina. Henry Killen moved to Neshoba County in 1832, just after the signing of the Treaty of Dancing Rabbit Creek, and was one of the founders of the town of Philadelphia, Mississippi.

In 1964, Edgar Ray Killen was a thirty-eight-year-old ordained Baptist preacher and owner of a local sawmill who had unsuccessfully run for sheriff of Neshoba County. He was committed to the "social separation" of the races. He especially hated interracial marriages, believing that the Bible condoned segregation in Genesis: "And God said, 'let the earth bring forth the living creature after his kind, cattle and creeping thing, and beast of the earth after his kind: and it was so.'"

Like Bowers, Killen had an evangelical mission: to destroy godless Communism and all those who wanted to end segregation of the races. "The first thing that a Communist has to do," he said years later, "is swear an oath that there's no Supreme Being." Jews and blacks were Communists and integrationists, he believed. "There's no question that [Martin Luther] King was a Communist." (After King was assassinated in Memphis, Tennessee, on April 4, 1968, Killen asked the FBI for the name of the killer so he could "shake his hand.")

It was Killen who received the Number 4 order from Bowers to eliminate Schwerner. (Chaney and Goodman were not targeted by Bowers; they were murdered because they were in the car with Schwerner on the night of June 21, 1964.) Killen was the Klansman notified by Deputy Sheriff Price late Sunday afternoon, June 21, 1964, that Schwerner and the others were in the Philadelphia jail and that the execution plan should be set in motion while they were locked up. He then coordinated the event: bringing a group of almost two dozen Lauderdale and Neshoba county Klansmen together, planning the attack and the burial of the bodies, and assigning tasks to all the men.

Mary Winstead, the author of *Back to Mississippi*, is a cousin of Killen. In her book, she wrote about him:

> I've never met Cousin Edgar Ray. But from everything I've read, I feel like I know him: a Kleagle for the White Knights of Mississippi. Recruiting Klansmen into the Lauderdale and Neshoba County Klaverns. On the lookout for a kid from New York. And then, on a June night in 1964, the night of his life, he's focused, careful, and busy. Buying rubber gloves and gassing up the cars. Gathering up the guns and ammunition. Making sure the burial site is ready. Finding someone to run the bulldozer. Handpicking just the right men. I felt sick.

The Preacher was not convicted in 1967 for participation in the conspiracy to murder the civil rights trio because one juror refused to convict the Baptist minister. The 11:1 hung jury allowed Killen to walk free from the courtroom. The lone holdout for acquittal told the other jurors that "she couldn't vote guilty against Edgar Ray Killen for one reason — she could never convict a preacher."

Bowers, who was convicted at that trial, said later that he was "quite delighted to be convicted and have the main instigator of the entire affair walk out of the courtroom a free man." To date, the state has not brought Killen to trial for his participation in the murders of Schwerner, Goodman, and Chaney. He still lives quietly in Neshoba County.

Bob Moses

"The [spring 1960] sit-ins woke me up," writes Bob Moses in his book, *Radical Equations*. He continues:

> Until then, my Black life was conflicted, I was a 26 year old teacher at Horace Mann, an elite private school in the Bronx, moving back and forth between the sharply contrasting worlds of Hamilton College, Harvard University, Horace Mann and Harlem. The sit-ins hit me powerfully, in my soul as well as in the brain. I was mesmerized by the pictures I saw almost every day on the front pages of the *New York Times* — young committed Black faces seated at lunch counters or picketing, directly and with great dignity, challenging white supremacy in the South. They looked like I felt.

It was these sit-ins by college students (who would, within six months, be among the founders of the SNCC) that led Moses to Mississippi in 1960. "And that trip," he writes, "changed my life. I returned to the state a year later and over the next four years, was transformed as I took part in the voter registration movement there."

Bob Moses is the antithesis of Sam Bowers. Born in 1935, Bob grew up in Harlem in New York City. He went to Stuyvesant High School and, in 1952, won a scholarship to Hamilton College in Clinton, New York, where he came into contact with the writings of the French existentialist Albert Camus. Moses said later that Camus's essential message to him was the "need to cease being a victim while at the same time not becoming an executioner." During the summers before his junior and senior years, Moses worked at Quaker-run educational centers in Europe and then in Japan.

He went to Harvard for graduate work in philosophy, focusing on mathematical logic, and earned his master's degree in June 1957. Illness in his family and the death of his mother forced Moses to leave graduate school and return to the city to care for his sick father. He started teaching there, and then later, in 1959, began work with Bayard Rustin, one of the CORE founders, to organize the Youth Movement for Integrated Schools.

With encouragement from Rustin, Moses went to work in the SCLC's Atlanta, Georgia, office in the summer of 1960. A year later he accepted an invitation from C. C. Bryant, the president of the Pike County, Mississippi, branch of the NAACP, to establish a voter registration program in McComb, Mississippi, a town of 13,000 located in the southwest corner of the state. Arriving in July 1961, he then became a member of SNCC.

For Moses, Mississippi was the "middle of the iceberg." After 1961, he spent most of his time traveling across the state setting up voter registration programs. During this time he met Amzie Moore, the president of the Cleveland, Mississippi, NAACP branch, located in the heart of the Mississippi Delta region. It was Moore who suggested to Moses that there was a need for a coordinating civil rights structure that could orchestrate the various activities of the small bands of civil rights workers laboring for SNCC, NAACP, CORE, and other groups. Moses, in turn, pushed for the creation of COFO and, in 1962, became its program codirector. Thereafter, civil rights workers were SNCC or CORE workers toiling together as COFO personnel.

In May 1964, he was in Washington, D.C., to testify in support of the proposed civil rights act. He told House legislators that the nation "was facing a situation in Mississippi that could be ten times worse than Birmingham," where the SCLC marchers were beaten, set upon by police dogs, hit with powerful water hose cannons, and arrested for protesting segregation.

As early as 1962, the secret investigators for the Sovereignty Commission were compiling data on this twenty-nine-year-old SNCC/ COFO leader. An April 22, 1963, report, written by Tom Scarbrough, had this to say about Moses:

Moses is the instructor for the trained agitators who are now agitating racial disorder throughout Mississippi. He has been known to work in the following counties: Amite, Walthall, Forrest, Lincoln, Hinds, Leflore, Sunflower, Washington, Coahoma, Marshall, and Bolivar. Shooting into houses and various charges of brutality have followed Moses wherever he goes. White racists are accused of being responsible for these alleged incidents; however, FBI agents, state and local authorities have not been able to place the blame on white people on any of the various charges. . . . At one time, he moved into Sunflower County and instigated a drive to register Negroes. A total of around 42 houses were fired into by someone . . . while Moses was busy trying to get Negroes to register to vote. . . . It is known that Robert Moses, Carl Braden, a known Communist, William Biggs, and Miles Horton (Negro Communist) held a voter registration seminar for Negroes at Tougaloo College and at the Christian Training Institute at Edwards, Mississippi in August, 1962. [It was] called "Operation Break-Through" meaning to tear down, trample, and destroy our state laws, customs, and traditions.

Scarbrough concluded the three-page report with the following observations:

Robert Moses has a way of showing up at various places in which there might be some racial strife. Moses has excellent contact with all news media. . . . From my experience by investigating Robert Moses' activities, I must conclude that he is working hand-in-glove with Communist sympathizers if not out-right Communist agitators. It is my opinion that Moses himself is a Communist; if he is not he is following the Communist line of operation.

Moses knew that for every COFO action, there was a much more violent white reaction. In the eyes of Sam Bowers, Preacher Killen, or Deputy Sheriff Cecil Price, there was no difference between a Freedom Ride project and a voter registration or Freedom School project. They were all the handiwork of the Antichrist disguised as Jews, blacks, Communists, and homosexuals. Driving outside Greenwood, Mississippi, in 1963, Moses and two companions were shot at by three men who pulled up alongside them and fired point-blank. One of the passengers, SNCC/COFO worker Jimmy Travis, was shot in the head and shoulder and narrowly escaped death. This, for Moses, was the reality that faced COFO personnel in 1960s Mississippi.

Mickey Schwerner

The CORE files in the Library of Congress contain a revealing letter, written on June 23, 1964, just a few days after Mickey Schwerner's disappearance (along with J. E. Chaney and Andy Goodman). The letter was sent from George Schiffer, a lawyer in New York City, to Judge Bernard Botein, the presiding judge of the Appellate Division, Supreme Court of New York State, First Department. It seems that during the previous summer, on July 14, 1963, Mickey, along with his wife, Rita, and other protesters, sat down in front of a truck on a construction site in New York County "to protest discrimination by unions in the construction industry against Negroes and Puerto Ricans." He was arrested for violating Section 722 of the penal code, tried, found guilty, and sentenced to the city prison workhouse for a period of sixty days. Prior to imposing sentence, the court engaged in the following colloquy with the defendant:

> THE COURT: Do you intend to continue this type of conduct of which you have been convicted? . . .
>
> DEFENDANT SCHWERNER: If it is deemed necessary to fight discrimination in this manner, I will have to do it, yes.

Schiffer then went to the reason for the letter to Judge Botein. He had been asked to appeal the disorderly conduct convictions of the married couple before they left for Mississippi. The matter was still pending when Mickey

> disappeared in or about Philadelphia, Mississippi. . . . I confess that I do not know how to proceed at this time. Mickey must be presumed dead, murdered. . . . He and his parents and his wife are entitled to have the erroneous conviction reversed. A pardon will not serve that purpose. I cannot conceive that it is the law of New York that Mickey Schwerner should go to his death convicted of disorderly conduct for affirming his beliefs in a positive, practical way.

The lawyer then presented Mickey's nonviolent philosophy to the judge:

> Mickey felt it is a duty, not a mere right, for the citizen to act in defense of constitutional principles. This duty, to support the Constitution, not merely to obey it, is laid upon our public officials, all attorneys. . . . From the founders of our nation to the architects of the Nuremberg trials, the obligation is laid upon the individual citizen to oppose lawless, unconstitutional or unnatural conduct on the part of constituted authorities.

Mickey Schwerner, like Bob Moses, was also born in New York City, although somewhat later, in November 1939. He was the second of two sons of a father who operated a wig manufacturing plant and a mother who taught in New York City's public schools. As an expression of his commitment to nonviolent social protest, he named his dog Gandhi.

Mickey graduated from Cornell University, with a major in rural sociology, in 1961 and took a job as a social worker in New York City. He married Rita Levant in June 1962, and the next year both joined CORE. In January 1964 the couple traveled from Manhattan to Meridian, Mississippi, by way of Jackson, Mississippi, where they met with and were briefed by Bob Moses. Schwerner was the first white CORE worker to be permanently placed in a city other than Jackson, Mississippi. (His salary was $9.60 a week.) He maintained that Mississippi was "the decisive battleground for America. Nowhere in the world is the idea of white supremacy more firmly entrenched, or more cancerous, than in Mississippi."

Quickly the married couple, with fellow CORE workers, established the Meridian Community Center and other programs, including voter registration classes. In late January Mickey successfully planned and implemented a black boycott of a local variety store whose customers were primarily blacks but that did not have any black employees. He had no problem interacting with the blacks in Meridian. Sue Brown, who worked with Mickey in 1964, recalled:

> More than any white person I have ever known he could put a colored person at ease. To a group of young Negroes he didn't seem like a preacher, or do-gooder, or a social worker, or somebody who

was out slumming, or a reporter who had come to learn about Negroes. He was the only white man I have ever known that you could associate with and forget he was white. He didn't talk down or up to you, he just talked to you. He made you feel he was interested in you, not because you were a Negro, but because you were folks too. He never pretended that he knew what was best for you.

By April 1964, two judgments had been made: Mickey believed that he made the right choice in coming to Mississippi to work for integration and voting rights for blacks; and Imperial Wizard Bowers issued a Number 4 order to Preacher Killen — eliminate Goatee. And, on the night of June 21, 1964, Mickey Schwerner was murdered.

Rita Schwerner remarked later: "He wanted to live; he loved life. He didn't want to die. . . . To save his life, I think he would have done anything within his physical power. Mickey was incapable of believing that a police officer in the United States would arrest him on a highway for the purpose of murdering him, then and there, in the dark." Much like learning about the characters in a Gothic novel, the reader has now met the perpetrators and the victims and has seen the values each held that propelled them to action and murderous reaction in Mississippi in the heartrending first six months of 1964. It is also important to recall the largest cohort in this tragedy: the bystanders. Many tens of thousands of white Mississippians — like other "silent majorities" throughout history — were frightened into silence in the face of brute lawlessness by a small number of terrorists. They were, however, brought up in a culture that emphasized social and intellectual inequality between the races. Most believed that whites were, as a race, superior to blacks and that segregation of the races was an appropriate social goal. They also believed that the beatnik, hippie-type civil rights workers were in reality part of a massive Communist conspiracy to destroy American values. At the same time, they were far from enamored with the violence brought down on the blacks and others by their more aggressive white neighbors, the KKKers.

CHAPTER 3

COFO's "Mississippi Freedom Summer" Project

The Battle Line Is Drawn

*We wanted to break Mississippi open. It was a kind of blitzkrieg. Previous to
that summer [1964], we had been weaving, trying to weave a network or a
community of people who could work to change the system. But it was so slow and
so many people were getting picked off one by one, the local leaders were getting
murdered, people were being evicted, and the white power structure was so strong
that it really seemed like we needed an enormous amount of outside support to
punch a hole in the whole system of segregation.*

CASEY HAYDEN, SNCC, 1972

*We were invaded by whores and Jews who tried to tell us how to run things.
Good people are killed every day in Mississippi, but the FBI only comes in on
it when worthless Jews and nigger-lovers are killed.*

WHITE ATTORNEY, PHILADELPHIA, MISSISSIPPI, AUGUST 1964

While there was massive resistance to federal court orders from the
moment *Brown* was announced on "Black Monday" in May 1954, including harassment, killings, and burnings, there was no organized Mississippi Klan presence in the state until the beginning of 1964. By that
time, the hard-core segregationists had concluded that the Mississippi
White Citizens Council was not doing an adequate job of thwarting
civil rights protesters and that civil rights personnel were brazenly
entering the Magnolia State in ever-greater numbers.

What triggered the push for the reincarnation of the White Knights
of the Mississippi Ku Klux Klan was the success of the fall 1963 COFO
"Freedom Votes" program and an announcement by COFO that there
would be a statewide Mississippi Freedom Summer program involving hundreds of civil rights volunteers working with thousands of black
Mississippi residents. For the white power structure in the state, this
was tantamount to an "invasion" of thousands of "beatniks, Commies,

niggers, and Jews" to try to destroy the venerable customs and traditions that had existed in Mississippi for more than a century.

The COFO plans had to be thwarted, and this goal became the leitmotiv and raison d'être of the Mississippi Klan. By the time the busloads of volunteers started to arrive in Mississippi in late June 1964, Klan membership had increased dramatically. At the Klan's inception in February 1964, it had about 300 members. By June 1964, according to FBI data, the number had grown to between 5,000 and 6,000 members operating in more than sixty of the state's eighty-two counties. The upsurge had a traumatic impact on the civil rights workers — veterans and volunteers alike. Sally Belfrage, one of the veterans of SNCC and the author of *Freedom Summer*, spoke for all of them: "You talk about fear — it's like the heat down here, it's continually oppressive. You think they're rational. But, you know, you suddenly realize they want to kill you."

That fear was like botulism in the Mississippi air. It infected many people — including the vast majority of Mississippians as well as the civil rights workers — and there really was no immediate cure for the malady: the silence brought on by the fear. Indeed, only those inoculated (the WCC and the KKK) or those who bested the infection spoke and acted, for good and evil. Consequently, because of the silence of the majority during this turbulent era in American history, the drama was played out by the vocal opponents, the Klan and the civil rights groups associated with COFO.

———

Triggering the Tragedy: The 1964 Mississippi Freedom Summer

"We wanted to break Mississippi open." Casey Hayden's words, which describe Freedom Summer as COFO's "blitzkrieg," capture the desperate necessity of developing some kind of major, statewide event that would simultaneously focus on the dilemma of the denial of black voting rights and capture the attention of the nation. Working on the success of the COFO-run fall 1963 "Freedom Vote: Campaign for Governor," in which more than 100 students from Yale and Stanford Universities worked to get more than 80,000 blacks to cast unofficial "freedom" ballots, COFO decided to amplify that program with one the following summer that would bring into the state ten times the number of volunteers from across the nation to help blacks register to vote in "real" elections.

Mississippi Freedom Summer was a bold move by COFO, one that directly challenged the segregationists on their hallowed ground. The summer program, directed by Bob Moses, had as its main objective trying to end the political disfranchisement of blacks in the state (and across the South). In 1964, whereas blacks constituted about 40 percent of the total population of Mississippi, only about 6.7 percent were registered voters, the lowest percentage in the nation.

It was nearly impossible for blacks to register to vote in Mississippi. At the clerk's office in the local courthouse, a prospective registrant who did not have proof of a sixth-grade education had to fill out a four-page, twenty-question "literacy" test. The clerk-registrar also gave each prospective registrant a section of the Mississippi Constitution to read and "reasonably" interpret. The answers were scored by the clerk; inevitably blacks failed the test, were declared "illiterate," and were not registered to vote.

The 1964 COFO voter registration drive, in the final analysis, was not successful. Only after KKK murders of voting rights workers in Alabama in 1965 did things change dramatically. In 1965 President Johnson asked Congress to pass a radical Voting Rights Act. Within three months, the bill was passed. By 1970, almost 65 percent of blacks were registered to vote in Mississippi.

While COFO was a confederation, SNCC wound up supplying personnel in four of the five Mississippi congressional districts. (CORE supported its staff only in the Fourth Congressional District, which included Canton, Philadelphia, and the Meridian operation run by Mickey Schwerner.) SNCC also provided 95 percent of the COFO personnel in the Jackson office and more than 90 percent of the operating funds to run the Freedom Summer programs throughout the state.

The critical component of the proposed program was the recruitment and mobilization of almost 1,000 college students from the North — mostly middle- and upper-class whites — to complement the black college students from southern colleges. In terms of public relations, this was a signal aspect of the COFO blitzkrieg, for it meant that hundreds of news reporters and television crews would visit the state as well.

There were some heated conversations about the appropriateness of having an integrated force of volunteers to implement the Freedom Summer projects. A few of the SNCC leaders argued for an all-black force of volunteers; others, including Bob Moses, felt it was important to recruit as many white students as possible to maximize publicity surrounding the project.

Moses acknowledged that "the space in the black community was really not a completely welcoming space. So there are some elements there which were welcoming them and bringing them into the family, but there was this resentment also, so they [the white volunteers] had to figure out how to walk through that. . . . What is to their ever-lasting credit is that they did." Moses' position won out, and by the end of June 1964, when the project began in Mississippi, more than 80 percent of the 900-plus volunteers were white students. However, the issue of white participation in these civil rights actions did not go away. By 1967, SNCC had become a radicalized group, one that barred all but blacks from participating in its actions.

Robbie Osman, one of the white college volunteers, addressed the unspoken reality that was an integral part of the summer project idea from the beginning:

> The very reason we were there as white college students was that unless the country's attention [was captured] by the presence of those people that this country was accustomed to caring about, namely white college students, nothing would happen. And if it was only people who this country was not accustomed to caring about, namely black Mississippians, then nothing would happen.

During the spring, the volunteers were sent reading lists ("read these three before coming South": *Souls of Black Folk*, by W.E.B. DuBois, *The Mind of the South*, by W. J. Cash, and *The Other America*, by Michael Harrington); a list of items to bring with them for their stay, and, ominously, power of attorney documents. They were told that $150 would cover a person's transportation, living, and personal need expenses "for the entire summer."

It would be wise, COFO informed them, "to make contacts with individuals or groups in your area who would be able to post bond for you in the event of arrest." All of the volunteers received a security handbook containing instructions on how to live and travel as safely as possible while working for civil rights in Mississippi. Among the warnings:

> No one should go anywhere alone, but certainly not in an automobile, and certainly not at night.
>
> Know locations of sanctuaries and safe homes in the county.
>
> When getting out of a car at night, make sure the car's inside light is out.
>
> If it can be avoided, try not to sleep near open windows.
>
> Try to avoid bizarre or provocative clothing, and beards. Be neat.
>
> No interracial groups traveling, day or night, unless absolutely necessary. And if that happened, whoever [is] in the minority must be hidden, covered with blankets, lying on the floor boards, whatever.

All these materials focused on one primary theme: The volunteers must be made aware of the world they were going to enter into that summer. SNCC staffer Hollis Watkins said: "We had to tell these young people exactly what they were really going to get involved in. They had to be prepared to go to jail, they had to be prepared to be beaten, and they had to be prepared to be killed. And if they were not prepared for either one or all three of those, then they should probably reconsider coming to Mississippi."

The summer volunteers would face a world in which some white faces represented a threat to their well-being. Dean Zimmerman, from North Dakota, one of the white COFO summer volunteers, remarked after his stay in Mississippi: "You came to see white faces as something to fear. As you encounter a white face, you immediately, your body takes on a whole different posture, your mind becomes very alert. You are constantly on the lookout for what you may have to do in a big hurry just to survive."

Another vital component of the Freedom Summer plan was the organization of the Mississippi Freedom Democratic Party (MFDP), which would challenge the credentials of the state's Democratic Party participants at the August 1964 Democratic National Convention in Atlantic City, New Jersey. In the end, more than 80,000 Mississippians joined the MFDP, electing a slate of sixty-eight delegates to challenge the seating of the regular — and all-white — Mississippi Democratic Party delegation. While the plan failed in 1964, it, too, brought national television coverage to the challenge and led the Democratic Party's Rules Committee to ban racially discriminatory state delegations in the future.

The college volunteers were asked by COFO to do the following:

> See if you can solicit the support of anyone you know who is close to the Democratic Party. Solicit their support for getting your state's delegation to support the challenge at the Democratic National Convention. Send any contacts you make to Casey Hayden at the COFO office. We must have Northern support for the challenge and your contacts may make the crucial difference.

More than thirty "Freedom Schools" were also established during Freedom Summer, and by the end of the summer, more than 3,000 black youngsters would be in attendance. These schools highlighted the deplorable state of secondary education — for both blacks and whites — in Mississippi's public schools. Many volunteers from the North taught remedial instruction in mathematics and reading, along with courses that examined the black experience in America.

The idea for the Freedom Schools was presented to the COFO summer program leaders in February 1964 by Charles Cobb. In a letter found in the COFO files at the Library of Congress, Cobb wrote:

> I would like to propose summer Freedom schools during the months of July and August for tenth- and eleventh-grade high school students in order to: 1. supplement what they aren't learning in high school around the state, 2. give them a broad intellectual and academic experience during the summer to bring back to fellow students in the state, and 3. form the basis for statewide student action such as a school boycott, based on their increased awareness.

Cobb — whose ideas were implemented during the summer of 1964 — also suggested a five-part curriculum for these schools: supplementary education (grammar, reading, typing, history, etc.); cultural programs such as art and music appreciation; political and social science, relating their studies to their environment; literature; and film programs.

In addition to the hundreds of "frontline" COFO volunteers and their veteran civil rights guides, about 100 CORE and SNCC workers (who were called "jungle fighters" by the volunteers training in Ohio), there was a supporting infrastructure that included doctors, dentists, nurses, photographers, entertainment, a chaplain corps, and the legal troops. The Medical Committee for Human Rights consisted of two white doctors and all fifty-seven black doctors practicing in Mississippi at the time. However, only two hospitals were available for use by COFO in the entire state.

There was also a World War II USO-type operation, the Mississippi Caravan of Music and the Free Southern Theatre, which visited all the COFO centers and Freedom Schools during the summer of 1964 to provide some kind of entertainment to the "troops." The National Council of Churches, one of the external sponsors of Freedom Summer, provided clergy — including rabbis and priests — to minister to the religious needs of the volunteers. Although there were 2,000 lawyers in Mississippi in 1964, only three black lawyers and one white lawyer were available to COFO. (The NAACP's LDF attorneys were not available because of a bitter ideological dispute that surfaced during the spring planning sessions.)

An April 1964 memo from Carl Rachlin of the New York office of CORE raised the problem: the ideological clash between the NAACP's LDF (fiercely anti-Communist and always frightened about the possibility of Communist Party infiltration of the organization) and COFO regarding the use of lawyers who were members of an organization allegedly allied with the Communist Party. (This problem existed for decades and was highly visible during the 1930s when the two legal organizations collided over representation for the "Scottsboro Nine" — the nine young black youngsters charged with rape of two white women, convicted, and sentenced to death in 1931.) As Rachlin wrote,

> Superimposed [on our political strategy regarding interactions with Democratic President Lyndon B. Johnson] is a major dispute brewing between the Legal Defense Fund [NAACP] on the one hand and COFO and the National Lawyers' Guild on the other. The other day [Jack] Greenberg flatly told Moses that under no circumstances would the Legal Defense Fund cooperate with the National Lawyers' Guild attorneys. Anticipating this [blowup,] we are at the moment engaged in a major effort, under my instigation

with the cooperation of the ACLU, National Council of Churches, Father Drinan [a Democratic congressman from Massachusetts], the American Jewish Committee, . . . to co-opt lawyers from all over the country to spend their vacation time trouble spotting in the South.

He concluded with a sage observation: "The mass presence of the Lawyers' Guild in Mississippi will unfortunately cause political hysteria. I have to persuade the Lawyers' Guild . . . to issue an anti-Communist statement."

The announcement by Moses of the Freedom Summer project also triggered intense, bitter, and immediate reaction by many members of the white community in Mississippi. For them, this was a Communist-Jew plot to destroy America. An editorial in the *Laurel* (Miss.) *Liberator* spoke for them:

A thousand college students from the North — attending inflammatory training schools — are reported to be invading Mississippi this summer in order to engage in a Negro voter registration drive. It is unbelievable that [they] would do this of their own volition. Those who know the ways of propaganda, especially of a Communist nature, probably correctly suspect that the idealism of some college youngsters has been taken advantage of by some very hard boiled left wingers and Communists who know exactly what they want to do — stir up trouble in the South. . . . The really serious aspect of this invasion is that it is part of an over-all scheme to destroy the United States by way of a racial revolution.

After June 1964, the volunteers, the Freedom Schools, the buildings COFO used as local headquarters in a city or town, and the persons and homes of local black residents who assisted COFO volunteers became targets of the Klan: twenty project offices, thirty black homes and businesses, thirty-seven churches were firebombed that summer; more than eighty volunteers were beaten by white mobs, and more than a thousand were arrested, held in jails, beaten, or otherwise "scared to death." And, of course, almost a dozen civil rights workers were murdered.

In the FBI files (No. 100–43190), the FBI account of the summer's Klan activities, entitled Bureau Monograph 1386, "Student Nonviolent Coordinating Committee," indicated that "at least 37 shootings [occurred and at least 6 murders of black civil rights volunteers *before* the summer began] while COFO volunteers were engaged in constitutionally protected activities during Freedom Summer."

One of the student volunteers wrote to his parents about a particular experience in Madison County, Mississippi, illustrating the ways segregationists struck back:

> We got about 14 Negroes to go to the court house with the intention of registering to vote. Sheriff Smith greeted the party with a six shooter drawn from his pocket, and said "Okay, who's first." After several seconds a man who had never before been a leader stepped up to the Sheriff, smiled and said "I'm first, Hartman Turnbow." All registration applications were permitted to be filled out and all were judged illiterate. The next week, Turnbow's house was bombed with Molotov cocktails. When the Turnbows left the burning house, they were shot at. A couple of days later, Turnbow was accused of having bombed his own house which wasn't insured. Sheriff Smith was the one witness against him. Mr. Turnbow was convicted.

As early as January 1964, after the formal announcement by Moses of the Mississippi Freedom Summer project, the Sovereignty Commission's investigators and their black informants and spies began to plan for the summer's activities. Some of the black "moles" attached themselves to COFO headquarters in Jackson, Mississippi. In June, other moles wound up in Oxford, Ohio, and circulated among the hundreds of volunteers to gather information for the MSSC.

The recently opened Sovereignty Commission files contain data showing that the moles sent to the commission the names of all the volunteers, the times the volunteers were going to travel to the state, and the towns and cities that the student volunteers were headed for. Also revealed was the fact that all this information collected by the Sovereignty Commission, including the license plate numbers of 136 cars used by COFO and others in the project, was given to both the White Citizens Council and the Mississippi KKK leaders.

During the months of January and February 1964, the three primary Sovereignty Commission investigators visited the sheriffs in all of Mississippi's eighty-two counties. Their task: provide the law enforcement officers with information regarding Mississippi state trespass laws and a two-page digest of relevant criminal codes. Later on, in May 1964, these investigators held a series of "night clinics" across Mississippi, preparing the sheriffs for the upcoming "invasion" of COFO volunteers.

Mickey and Rita Schwerner Come to Meridian, Mississippi

As soon as Mickey arrived at the Meridian CORE office front, he took charge. Also, soon after he arrived, Schwerner was under constant surveillance by Lauderdale and Neshoba County Klansmen. He held training sessions for volunteers who were in Mississippi to help blacks prepare for the literacy test they had to take in order to register to vote. He created a community center in the office as a place where blacks could congregate. He tutored black residents who cautiously agreed to try to register to vote.

By the end of May 1964, there were twelve paid CORE staff members in all of Mississippi, counting Mickey and Rita Schwerner. They were located in the major towns and cities in Mississippi's Fourth Congressional District: Meridian, Philadelphia, and Canton. In May, the CORE staff in the state broke the district into two sections — east and west. Schwerner was the director of the eastern section, which included Newton, Lauderdale, Kemper, Neshoba, Clarke, and Jasper Counties.

In a May 27, 1964, letter to the New York headquarters of CORE, a request was made by Schwerner to fund an additional eight staff, including J. E. Chaney, who at the time was an unpaid volunteer working with Mickey in Meridian, Mississippi. CORE was readying its small organization for the influx of volunteers from the North who were coming down in a month. Planned for the district were voter registration drives in all the counties and Freedom Schools in Meridian (2), Neshoba (1), and Clarke (1) Counties. In the letter, Mickey made the following request to cover the costs of the planned activities of the twelve-week Freedom Summer projects:

Food (staff)	$ 960.00
Telephones	250.00
Utilities	175.00
Rent at Freedom Houses	360.00
Freedom Schools	895.00
Community Center (Meridian)	370.00
Sub total #1	3,010.00

I need a credit card for gas. . . . [I] would also like to get at least three more cars for the summer project. Please answer soon. In the name of FREEDOM. . . .

Mickey quickly became very close to one of the volunteers in the Meridian office, James Earl "J. E." Chaney, who soon traveled with him to visit the black communities across the eastern section of the Fourth Congressional District. Chaney, the son of a plasterer, was born in Meridian in May 1943. He was an early civil rights activist who once had been suspended from his all-black school for wearing an NAACP pin to classes and began doing volunteer work in the Meridian office of CORE in 1963. When Mickey arrived in late January 1964, he was immediately impressed with J. E.'s knowledge and skills and recommended Chaney for a full-time post with CORE.

"Goatee" Is Targeted for "Elimination"

A few days after the budget letter was sent, on May 30, 1964, Mickey and J. E. traveled to the Mount Zion Methodist Church, a black church eight miles east of Philadelphia, Mississippi. They visited with the deacons of the church to see if COFO volunteers could use the building as a training center for voter registration sessions over the next twelve weeks.

This was a fateful, tragic trip for the two men. Unbeknownst to them, by this time Sam Bowers, aware of Mickey's energetic leadership, had instructed the Lauderdale and Neshoba county Klaverns to activate plan Number 4: the target, "Goatee."

Although six blacks had already been murdered by the Klan in Mississippi since March, Schwerner was an especially bright target. He was an aggressive white civil rights leader, someone who had the respect of all the blacks who met or worked with him. He was a charismatic Antichrist, thought Bowers; he had to be eliminated.

Bob Stringer, a teenager working for Bowers at the Sambo Amusement Company office in 1964, attended several Klan meetings in April 1964. At the first meeting, Bowers spoke to the Lauderdale and Neshoba County Klansmen about the upcoming Freedom Summer. "We are here," he said, "to discuss what we are going to do about COFO's nigger-communist invasion of Mississippi, which will begin in a few days. . . . Any personal attacks on the enemy should be carefully planned to include only the leaders and prime white collaborators of the enemy forces."

At a small meeting later in the month, attended by Bowers, Killen, Stringer, and one other unidentified person, Bowers told Edgar Ray Killen to "eliminate" Schwerner. Bowers said, "Goatee is like the queen bee in the beehive. You eliminate the queen bee and all the workers go away."

The Mississippi Freedom Summer Volunteers Arrive for "Boot Camp" in Oxford, Ohio

On June 14, 1964, the first 200 volunteers of the more than 900 students who eventually participated in Freedom Summer arrived on the campus of the Western College for Women in Oxford, Ohio, for their weeklong training, which was financed and sponsored by the National Council of Churches. The COFO volunteers were on that campus preparing for the reality of being interlopers in Mississippi. These volunteers, the greatest number of whom were white (by a 5:1 ratio) and 40 percent of whom were female, came from campuses across the nation, including Berkeley, Harvard, Radcliffe, Cornell, CUNY, Princeton, Stanford, Wisconsin, and the University of Chicago. Most were between twenty and twenty-five years of age; they came from affluent, prominent families. One of the volunteers was the son of Congressman Don Edwards (D-Calif.). "You're going to be classified into two groups in Mississippi," said J. R. Brown, one of the small number of black attorneys practicing in Mississippi, to the gathering, "niggers and nigger-lovers, and they're tougher on nigger-lovers."

In attendance, too, were the "moles" in the employ of the MSSC.

Almost on a daily basis they sent informative reports to the commission's executive director about the goings-on at the Ohio training site. One such report, dated June 19, 1964, identified the locations of the Freedom Schools, reported on the speech givers at the general session meeting held that day, described the purposes of the special orientation classes, and gave detailed information on the transportation used by the volunteers traveling to Mississippi. "The National Lawyers Guild and the National Council of Churches appear to be the principal forces behind this program," wrote the informant in his report. Attached to the report were copies of the literature handed out by COFO.

Another report, dated June 22 and 23, 1964, noted that in addition to the hundreds of American students attending the sessions, there were also students from Japan, France, Switzerland, India, and England in attendance. Students were warned by speaker after speaker, the letter continued, "that some of them might be killed or maybe beaten up, so [they] urged [the students] to notify their senators and congressmen of their activities." The student volunteers "were not going to participate in any sit-ins or demonstrations." They would, instead, "teach some Negroes how to read and write" in the Freedom Schools.

One of the featured speakers was a forty-three-year-old Minnesota native, John Doar, the deputy chief of the Department of Justice's Civil Rights Division, who had assisted James Meredith in his effort to enroll in the University of Mississippi in 1962. Doar had worked at Justice for four years, since 1960. In 1961 he became the alter ego and deputy chief to Burke Marshall (the chief of the Civil Rights Division). He was in Ohio to represent U.S. Attorney General Robert Kennedy. After reading a statement prepared by Kennedy, Doar welcomed questions from those in attendance.

Doar's response to a question from one of the volunteers set off a near riot. "What are you [the federal government, the Department of Justice, and the FBI] going to do to enable us to see this fall?" asked the young college student. Doar answered, "Nothing. There is no federal police force. The responsibility for [your] protection is that of the local Mississippi police. We can only investigate." One of the CORE veterans then said to Doar and to the volunteers: "[In other words], if you go, you can die." Bedlam broke out at that point, according to Len

Holt, one of the veteran civil rights lawyers present. Questions from angry, frightened volunteers followed one after another regarding the ability and responsibility of the federal government to protect them from being beaten up or murdered.

Doar did not budge from his initial answer. There was no federal police force. The use of troops by the president was a last resort in the face of rioting and imminent threats of injury and death — Little Rock, Arkansas; Montgomery, Alabama; and Oxford, Mississippi, were the exceptions. Only when something tragic occurred — or was about to happen — could the federal government enter the picture.

Doar was extremely sympathetic with the goals and objectives of COFO and the volunteers. "I admire what you intend to do," he told the volunteers in Ohio. When, in 1967, the Klansmen were brought to trial in federal court, he was the lead prosecutor in the government's case against them. However, in Ohio in late June 1964, he echoed the beliefs of FBI director J. Edgar Hoover, who was not at all enamored of the activities of these civil rights organizations. In November 1963, Hoover said brusquely, "We don't guard anyone. We do not wet nurse those who go down to reform the South." While many of those attending the training session were extremely angry at Doar's response — an anger that increased exponentially when news of the "disappearance" of the three civil rights workers was announced — very few of the 900 or more volunteers actually quit the program and returned home.

Among the 100 CORE and SNCC veteran "jungle fighters" attending the training sessions were Mickey Schwerner and J. E. Chaney. They planned to stay there for part of a week and then take the volunteers for the Meridian projects down with them in Mickey's station wagon. That plan never saw the light of day, however, because of the trap the Klan had set to lure Mickey Schwerner back to Neshoba County — and to his death.

Laying the Trap for Mickey — and Murdering Him and His Colleagues

On June 16, two days after the first volunteers arrived in Oxford, Ohio, a large meeting of Lauderdale and Neshoba County Klansmen was held in the Boykin Methodist Church, just four miles east of Philadelphia. More than seventy new members were present. Presiding over the meeting was "Preacher" Killen, who that evening set in motion the plan for eliminating Goatee that would be accomplished five days later.

A group of the Klansmen drove to the Mount Zion Methodist Church with the hope of catching Schwerner there. That evening the black church group was deciding whether to allow COFO to use the building as a Freedom School as well as a training center for preparing blacks to register. The Klansmen rousted the blacks from the church, surrounded all the church elders, and beat a number of them. Later in the evening, frustrated that Goatee had not been at the church, they returned and firebombed the church, hoping that would bring Schwerner back to Mississippi to investigate.

Mickey did not hear about the beatings and the burning of the Mount Zion Church for a few days because the newspapers in the state, including the *Jackson Clarion Ledger*, chose not to print the story at all. Documents from the files of the Sovereignty Commission explain why the story never ran: both the *Clarion Ledger* and its sister paper, the *Jackson Daily News*, killed the story (and many others) at the request of the Sovereignty Commission or the White Citizens Council.

Sovereignty Commission investigator Hopkins, according to the commission files, asked T. V. Gamblin, a Philadelphia banker, why the FBI knew about the burning of the church but the locals, including the sheriff and the COFO leaders, did not. Gamblin's response, in Hopkins's report to the commission file, was as follows:

> He was partially responsible for keeping this matter reasonably quiet as an industrialist from New Jersey was in Philadelphia on Wednesday after the church burned on Tuesday night for the purpose of possibly locating a new industry in Neshoba County and that he, Mr. Gamblin, contacted the *Clarion Ledger* and asked them not to publish anything regarding the burning of the church, as he felt that it might have some bearing on whether the new industry located in Philadelphia. [The newspaper did not run the story.]

Mickey Schwerner read about the church burning some days later in a Louisiana newspaper. Bill Minor, a Mississippian who was a courageous news stringer in Mississippi for the *Times-Picayune* in New Orleans, was tipped off about the incident and spoke to some of the locals in and around Philadelphia; the newspaper ran the story a few days after the event occurred. As soon as he read the story, Mickey quickly changed his plans so he could drive back to Meridian with J. E. to visit the site of the church burning. He took along a number of the young white volunteers, including twenty-year-old Andy Goodman, also from New York City.

Goodman's mother recalled her thoughts when Andy told his parents about volunteering to work in Mississippi during the summer: "Here was our son wanting to go into the belly of the beast." Andy Goodman came from an affluent family who lived on the Upper West Side of Manhattan. Andy was fourteen and a student at the elite private Walden School in Manhattan when he participated in his first civil rights protest, a trip to Washington, D.C., to participate in the CORE-sponsored Youth March for Integrated Schools. (Bob Moses had participated in the same activity a few years before Andy.) In his senior year at Walden, Andy visited a depressed area of West Virginia to write a report about the poor state of coal miners' lives. In April 1964, after listening to a speech given on campus by liberal Democratic congressman Allard Lowenstein, Andy decided to apply for work in the Mississippi Freedom Summer project.

In 1964 Andy, twenty years old, attended Queens College of the City University of New York (CUNY). He was majoring in anthropology and had joined SNCC a few years earlier. His parents held very liberal political beliefs, and growing up in that environment enabled Andy to meet interesting visitors to the Goodman apartment, including the controversial Alger Hiss, blacklisted actor Zero Mostel, and Martin Popper, the attorney who represented the "Hollywood Ten" (a group of Hollywood screenwriters blacklisted because of their alleged associations with communists).

Goodman was scheduled to do his Freedom Summer work in Canton, Mississippi, but changed his mind when Mickey asked for a volunteer to accompany the two veteran civil rights workers when they went back to Lauderdale County. On June 19 Andy called his parents to tell them of his change in plans. Immediately after the call, the trio — along with five volunteers who were assigned to the Meridian COFO voter registration and Freedom School projects — drove all night and day, arriving in Meridian on Saturday, June 20.

The next day — Father's Day — Schwerner, Chaney, and Goodman left Meridian for Philadelphia to investigate the burning of the church and the beatings of some of the church elders. Schwerner felt responsible for the events because of his visit with the church deacons three weeks earlier. On their way back to Meridian, about 2:00 P.M., traveling South on Highway 19, with J. E. driving, they were stopped for speeding by Deputy Sheriff Cecil Price.

Taken to the Neshoba County jail, they spent six or more hours while Price allegedly had to find a local magistrate to deal with Chaney's speeding ticket. There was never any need to involve the local magistrate — it was just a ruse to keep the civil rights trio in jail for many hours while the Klansmen planned for their murders later that night. Price, who told Schwerner and Goodman that he was "investigating" them, instead called Rainey and Killen to inform them that Schwerner was in jail and would remain there until after 10:00 P.M. As Price planned, the three men left the jail around 10:30 P.M. after Chaney paid the twenty-dollar speeding ticket.

At this point Mickey violated a fundamental COFO safety rule. He did not call either the CORE office in Meridian or the one in Jackson, Mississippi, to report on what had happened to them and to say that they were running very late. In all probability, he had no time to make such a call late at night. It was necessary to get the hell out of Philadelphia quickly, and besides, he simply did not know where a local public telephone might be in the small, unfamiliar city. So the trio quickly got into the station wagon and, escorted by Deputy Sheriff Price to the city line, returned to Highway 19 to continue their trip back to their office and homes in Meridian, about thirty-five miles to the southeast.

According to the confession of James Jordan, one of the Klansmen who participated in the killings, Deputy Sheriff Price stopped the three men again, placed them in his car, and then took them to the desolate, dirt Rock Cut Road, a right turn off Highway 19. There Killen's Klansmen — but not Killen himself, who left to attend a funeral — were waiting to eliminate Schwerner. "Goatee" was their target; the others just happened to be riding with him that day.

Preacher Killen was the planner and organizer of that night's murders. He met with Klansmen in the late afternoon, after Price brought the trio to the jail, at the Longhorn Drive-In in Meridian. Later that night, he met with the Klansmen who were to do the killings, at Akin's Mobile Homes, also in Meridian.

Killen made dozens of calls to Klansmen in both counties and set a time for the Klansmen to gather in Philadelphia, 8:15 P.M., to go over the final plans for the murders. He told them where to wait for the trio (who would be driven to the spot by Price); found brown cloth gloves for the murderers to wear; and located a spot for burying Schwerner and the others, as well as a Klansman to work the bulldozer. "We have a place to bury them, and a man to run the dozer to cover them up," Killen told Klansman Horace Doyle Barnette hours before the three young men were released from the jail. (Barnette was one of three Klansmen who confessed to the FBI and signed written confessions. Two other Klansmen became FBI informants.) After setting up the murders, the Preacher did not participate in the actual event; instead, he went to a local funeral home in Philadelphia to say words over the body of his dead uncle. Staff members in the Meridian CORE office expected Schwerner and the others to return to the office in the late afternoon. Soon staffers in the SNCC Atlanta office had been informed about the incipient problem. By late evening, the trio was greatly overdue, and around 12:30 A.M., Mary King, an Atlanta-based SNCC staffer, called Justice's John Doar at his home in Chevy Chase, Maryland. King told Doar, who had been in Ohio a week earlier talking to the volunteers, about the missing men and sought his help. By the following day, the FBI was at work investigating the disappearance of the three men.

Autopsy reports later revealed that J. E. was severely beaten and tortured by the Klansmen before he was finally killed. His left arm was broken in one place, and his right arm in two places; he had a broken jaw; he had also suffered trauma to the groin area. He was shot three times, Schwerner and Goodman were each killed with one bullet. One Klansman, Wayne Roberts, a twenty-six-year-old dishonorably discharged U.S. Marine, was the shooter, killing first Schwerner, then Goodman — both killed by shots to the heart — and then Chaney, the first two at point-blank range. According to Jordan, the Klansman who was at the scene of the killing and who confessed to the FBI, before Schwerner was fatally shot by Roberts, he said, "Sir, I know just how you feel." Additionally, Jordan said that Chaney was killed forty feet away from the other two men. This account meshed with a Sovereignty Commission report about the killings.

Andy Hopkins, a commission investigator, noted in his January 26,

1965, report to the Jackson office: "James Chaney, the colored member of this group, is alleged to have broke away from the group of men that were holding them captive. Shortly after he made the break, he was shot at several times by different people but was struck by only three bullets, each of which was alleged to have been fired from a different firearm."

After the bodies were disposed of, Deputy Sheriff Price spoke to the group:

> Well, boys, you've done a good job. You've struck a blow for the White Man. Mississippi can be proud of you. You've let those agitating outsiders know where this state stands. Go home now and forget it. But before you go, I'm looking each one of you in the eye and telling you this: "the first man who talks is dead! If anybody who knows anything about this ever opens his mouth to any outsider about it, then the rest of us are going to kill him just as dead as we killed those three sonofbitches tonight. Does everybody understand what I'm saying. The man who talks is dead, dead, dead!"

Buford Posey was a rarity in Philadelphia — indeed, in all of Mississippi. The native of Neshoba County was the first white man to join a Mississippi NAACP branch. He was active in civil rights at this time and had warned Mickey about the Klan's hatred of him. "I told him to be careful," he recalled years later. Around 2:00 A.M. on June 22, hours after the Klansmen killed the three men, Posey received a call from Edgar Ray Killen, who spoke briefly: "We took care of your three friends tonight and you're next!" Posey spoke to the FBI the following day, first to the agents in Jackson and then by phone to the bureau's New Orleans office. "I told them I was a civil rights worker, who I worked for and what had happened. I told them the preacher's name and that I thought the sheriff's office was involved in the murder[s]." For reasons unknown, however, he did not testify in the federal trial in 1967.

The civil rights workers never returned to Meridian, Mississippi. The trio vanished that night, and the following day, Monday, June 22, their burned-out car was found near the edge of the Bogue Chitto Swamp on the Choctaw Indian reservation. Evidently, Killen's plan had gone awry. The car, a 1963 blue Ford station wagon, was to be driven to Birmingham, Alabama, and disposed of there. Instead, the Klansmen drove the car about twenty-five miles northeast on Highway 21, entered the Choctaw Indian Reservation, set the vehicle on fire, then pushed it into the Bogue Chitto Swamp. They thought the car would never be found in that desolate spot. They were wrong. Had the car been driven, according to the plan, to the large city of Birmingham and disposed of there, the bodies of the three civil rights workers probably never would have been found.

FBI Special Agent John Proctor, working out of Meridian, Mississippi, received a telephone call from Lonnie Hardin, the superintendent of the Indian Agency on the Choctaw reservation, urgently asking the agent to meet him at the agency. When Proctor arrived, he was told that several Choctaws had found a smoldering station wagon off Highway 21 in the swamp. A man's watch but no bodies were found in the car. It was Mickey's watch, which had stopped keeping time at 12:45 A.M. Proctor immediately informed Washington of the discovery.

A massive search began at once, ordered by President Johnson and Attorney General Kennedy. Kennedy's Department of Justice treated the disappearance as a kidnapping to enable the FBI to enter the case. Within weeks, more than 150 special agents were assigned to the case of the missing civil rights workers. They received absolutely no cooperation from most of the Neshoba County residents. Instead, the FBI and others investigating the incident were met with what one agent called the "resistance of silence. . . . A wall of silence [was erected], born out of fear, suspicion, and open hostility."

Hundreds of sailors from the nearby Meridian Naval Air Station joined the federal investigators in the fruitless effort to find and recover the bodies of the three young men. The locals hated these federal intrusions into the quiet life of Mississippians. Most had no sympathy for the three missing young men and joked about the federal efforts to find them. One Neshoba County resident, watching sailors trawl the waters of the Bogue Chitto Swamp for the bodies of the civil rights workers, yelled to one group, "Hey, why don't you hold a welfare check out over the water. That'll get that nigger to the surface."

Up north in Oxford, Ohio, the news of the disappearance of the three men caused an understandable "flurry of activity," wrote one of the Sovereignty Commission moles. "Students are receiving emergency phone calls from their relatives, evidently urging them to withdraw from the program. I know of four (4) students who have left already. Prior to the burning of the church at Philadelphia, they were planning on conducting a Freedom school there. That is doubtful now." The mole evidently befriended some of the veteran civil rights workers as well as young volunteers. "One of the leaders," wrote the informant, "rode up to Oxford with the writer and will return with him. He is a white youth who appears to be very much of a radical. Also traveling with me is one Iris Greenberg, a White girl from New York." These paid informants were operating all over the state as well, providing detailed information about the plans being formulated by COFO.

Responses to the "Disappearances"

Walter Cronkite's six o'clock news broadcast on CBS-TV on June 25, 1964, led off with the main story sweeping America, the disappearance of the three civil rights workers. Cronkite described the disappearance — and the recovery of the charred station wagon — as being "the focus of the whole county's concern." Other national broadcast and television networks duplicated these stories about the men.

For the missing men's families, the forty-four-day wait until the bodies were found was "nothing but a horror," wrote Jerry Mitchell many years later in the *Jackson Clarion-Ledger*. J. E.'s brother Ben told Mitchell that "people called and threatened my mother's life and threatened to bomb the house. Crosses burned on the lawn. The house was shot in a couple of times. They fired her from her job."

The Schwerner family in Pelham, New York, received countless crank calls. And Andy Goodman's mother recalls the phone ringing regularly.

> Crank calls. Hate calls. Others said, "They're a couple of Jewish boys. What are they doing hanging out with black people?" [Goodman's mother recalled calls that demanded a ransom to get her son back.] "We know you're rich, and we know you have a lot of money and diamonds," she recalled them saying. "You know, $5,000 isn't much for your boy's life." It was really horrendous because you just wondered, "Could it be true? Could there be some terrorists holding on to the kids and just wanting money?"

This cruel psychological torture continued until the bodies were discovered in early August.

All three families demanded to see the governor of Mississippi and the president of the United States. Secretly, without informing the president or the attorney general, J. Edgar Hoover had FBI agents place wiretaps on the phones of the Schwerner, Chaney, and Goodman families. The FBI agents were able to hear and transcribe all calls they made externally, as well as all calls between the members of these families.

The response to the disappearance at the training camp in Oxford, Ohio, was equally emotional. Bob Moses recalled how the news of the three men's disappearance and death hit all the participants. Their murders (everybody on the campus in Ohio, in their guts, knew they were dead), he recalled, "set the tone of the training." The news, for the veterans, forced them "to make all the volunteers understand what they are about to get into," Moses said. "You can't whitewash this; you can't rose-color it in any way. You have to make them understand — because this is their last chance to get out."

> [The "disappearance"] took the whole training and the [Freedom] summer to a different space, I think, for those of us who were part of the organizing force and for those who had come to work with us, and so it really took it into a different emotional space and a different level of commitment. I think for people who weren't sure why they had come, I think that forced them to begin to understand better why they had come and what was at stake.

Judy Richardson, one of the young SNCC "jungle fighters" (she had started work in Mississippi almost one year earlier), was present when Moses made the announcement. She recalled "with clarity" the atmosphere many years later. Moses walked onto the stage in front of the students.

> He was very quiet, very Zen-like. Bob said that these three were missing. We all assumed that that meant they were dead. . . . The second morning, Bob came back on and he wrote on the blackboard "The three are still missing," and the next day — "The three are still missing." It was very hard, particularly for the students who had never worked in Mississippi and were just coming down for

the summer. It was like a slap of reality that this really could happen, that you really could be killed.

James Farmer, the national director of CORE, sent a letter on June 29, 1964, to the parents of the 900 volunteers who were already working in Mississippi:

> As a parent of a civil rights worker in Mississippi, you are doubtless even more shocked and upset than I am over the disappearance of CORE staffers James Chaney, Michael Schwerner, and student volunteer Andrew Goodman on the night of June 21st. On numerous occasions, I and other officers of CORE have pleaded with Robert Kennedy and other officials of the Department of Justice to offer federal protection to persons in the Freedom Summer project. Only a week before the Mississippi tragedy, Jim Peck, the Freedom Rider so severely beaten in 1961, asked Burke Marshall, the head of the Civil Rights Division: "Does somebody have to be killed before the Federal government intercedes?"

Farmer had arrived in Mississippi on June 25 with a delegation of more than forty blacks, including John Lewis, the young chairman of SNCC; George Raymond, CORE's Mississippi field secretary; and Dick Gregory, the comedian, "to see what I can do to bring justice in this case." Farmer requested the parents "to write to President Johnson as a parent and demand that your son or daughter receive adequate federal protection this summer in their work to make the principles for which we stand a reality in the deep south."

Letters began flooding the White House demanding that the federal government protect the workers and find the persons responsible for the disappearance of the three young men in or around Philadelphia, Mississippi. Actor E. G. Marshall and the entire cast and crew of the then-popular television show *The Defenders* wrote President Johnson demanding that "justice is done" in the tragedy. Major civil rights leaders, including representatives of CORE, SNCC, SCLC, and NAACP, flooded to Philadelphia, Mississippi, to buoy the spirits of the COFO personnel and the local black community.

White Mississippi and southern responses were quite different. People repeatedly argued, without batting an eye, that the disappearance was a hoax, a "publicity stunt," and that the trio was hiding out somewhere in the country or were, according to Mississippi's governor, Paul Johnson, taking in the sun "in Cuba." (It was Governor "Stand Tall with Paul" Johnson who told the press, during his successful campaign in 1963 that NAACP meant "niggers, apes, alligators, coons, and possums.") Letters and calls came into the FBI office in Jackson suggesting similar scenarios. And Robert Shelton, the National Grand Wizard of the KKK, also arrived in Philadelphia, Mississippi, to conduct his own private investigation of the disappearance of the trio.

Ironically, even the Neshoba County Sheriff's Office received letters. Six days after the trio was murdered, Sheriff Rainey's office in Philadelphia received a postcard from Detroit, Michigan, that read, "Call off your hunt. The boys are here with me—James, Andy, and Mickey. The boys only wonted [*sic*] a little fun." (After the bodies were found, Rainey was flooded with hundreds of letters congratulating him on his role in the murders of the young men. One said: "To men like you, Mr. Price, Mr. Beckwith, I take my hat off to you all." Another: "Mr. Rainey, I would be proud to be a member of your group. I know you all to be men, and I love each of you as a brother.")

A day after the disappearance became news, Mississippi's senior U.S. senator, Jim Eastland, spoke with President Johnson on the telephone:

LBJ: Jim, we got three kids missing down there. What can I do about it?

JE: I don't know. I don't believe there's three missing. I believe it's a publicity stunt. I'll tell you why I don't think there's a damned thing to it. . . . There's not a KKK in the area. There's not a WCC in that area. There's no organized white man in that area. Who could possibly harm them?

Mississippi's other senator was Democrat John C. Stennis, whose hometown was DeKalb, in the county adjacent to Lauderdale County. After Johnson spoke with Eastland, he discussed the disappearance with Stennis, whose take was somewhat different than that of his senatorial colleague: "I'm awfully worried about it, Lyndon, you know. [Chaney] has been making himself obnoxious—smart-aleck troublemaker—and I'm afraid someone is after him and just got the others along with him."

Johnson replied, "I just wanted you to know . . . my friend, and I sure love you and I know that your heart is bleeding [for Mississippi] and mine is too and maybe somehow we'll work out of this."

The Sovereignty Commission position was that the disappearance was a hoax. One of its investigators, Andy Hopkins, reported on June 29 that "the people in Philadelphia are extremely upset over this [bad publicity]. Most of the businessmen and good citizens still believe that this is a hoax perpetrated by the missing parties. Other people believe that it was a hoax to start with but are beginning to fear that these subjects have met with foul play."

In late July, three weeks after the young men disappeared, Senator Eastland said to a reporter:

> Many people in our state assert that there is just as much evidence, as of today, that they are voluntarily missing as there is that they have been abducted. No one wants to charge that a hoax has been perpetrated, because there is too little evidence to show just what did happen. But as time goes on, and the search continues, if some evidence of a crime is not produced, I think the people of America will be justified in considering other alternatives more valid solutions to the mystery, instead of accepting as true the accusation of the agitators that a heinous crime has been committed.

Burke Marshall, the assistant attorney general, Civil Rights Division, DOJ, was appointed by President Kennedy in 1961. From the beginning, Marshall — born in Plainfield, New Jersey — brought to his work a deep commitment to maintaining a viable federalism in the area of law enforcement. He well understood that local law enforcement officers in the South were frequently Klansmen who thought nothing of depriving civil rights workers of their fundamental rights and liberties. "I do not believe," he said in February 1965, in testimony before the U.S. Commission on Civil Rights, "the situation, deplorable as it may be in many parts [of the South], warrants departure from this historic pattern of limited federal power." Short of creating a national police force — which Congress would never agree to do — the federal government did not have the manpower to assume the responsibility for protecting civil rights workers across the nation.

For the taciturn Marshall, the federal government's role in dealing with the murder of citizens was minimal: there was no federal criminal statute that made such actions a crime. Further, the state's law enforcement machinery was the fundamental response to such capital offenses. What he tried to avoid at all costs was the perception that federal government operatives — soldiers, marshals, DOJ lawyers — were the "occupying power" in the South and would remain a very visible presence there until segregation and racial discrimination ended.

Although Marshall introduced more civil rights lawsuits than his Republican predecessors, he preferred to negotiate with southern political and business leaders to achieve desegregation of public and private facilities. In 1962, his approach led to the admission of James Meredith to the University of Mississippi. In 1963, his negotiation skills led to a settlement between SCLC leaders and Birmingham's business community that ended street demonstrations, police violence, and the use of police dogs against black marchers. The obituary for Marshall in the *New York Times* (he died in June 2003) noted that "his deft touch eased ticklish situations, enabling him, for instance, to warn Dr. King privately of the possibility that communists could infiltrate his following, and to elicit the secret help of Southern lawyers."

The federal government's response to the disappearance of Schwerner, Chaney, and Goodman was immediate and disconcerting. Less than a day after the men were reported missing, Burke Marshall's minions met in Jackson, Mississippi, to discuss the federal response. A Sovereignty Commission investigator attended the briefing given by a DOJ lawyer along with FBI agent John Proctor. His report stated that "they did not feel they had the authority to become involved in the search for the three workers. They said they were not sure a federal statute had been violated."

However, John Doar overrode their initial decision — with Burke Marshall's approval. After receiving information at 12:30 A.M. from a SNCC staff member in Atlanta, Georgia, saying that Schwerner and the others were long overdue from their trip to the Mount Zion Methodist Church, he immediately contacted Attorney General Robert Kennedy and his boss, Marshall. Doar was able to convince them that the federal Lindbergh Kidnapping Law enabled the FBI to enter the crisis to investigate and take any action necessary to apprehend the kidnappers.

President Johnson's audiotapes indicate that he did all he could, before and after the trio's disappearance, to get a massive FBI presence in Mississippi seen by the segregationists and the civil rights organizations. In a June 23 conversation with Lee White, associate counsel to the president, Johnson said:

> I asked Hoover two weeks ago to fill up Mississippi with FBI men and infiltrate everything [the KKK] he could, that they haul 'em in by the dozens. I've asked him to put more men after these three kids. . . . I'm shoving as much as I know how. . . . I didn't ask them to go and I can't control the actions of Mississippi people. The only weapon I have for locating 'em is the FBI. I haven't got any state police, or constables. And FBI is better than marshals and I've got all of 'em I've got looking after 'em. I can't find 'em myself.

That same day Johnson discussed the Mississippi crisis with Speaker of the House John McCormack (D-Mass.):

> LBJ: About three weeks ago, I called in Hoover and told him to fill Mississippi — I can't say this publicly — but load it down with FBI men and put 'em in every place they anticipate they can as informers and put 'em in the Klan and infiltrate it — we can't advertise this. . . . I don't want to be appearing to be directing this thing and appear that I'm invading the state and taking the rights of the Governor or Mayor.
>
> JMcC: In a day or two [the FBI] will catch those three. They can't disappear forever, can they?
>
> LBJ: No, unless they've killed them.

Later that day, Johnson spoke with Deputy U.S. Attorney General Nicholas Katzenbach:

> LBJ: What do you think happened to 'em?
>
> NK: I think they got picked up by some of these Klan people, would be my guess.
>
> LBJ: And murdered?
>
> NK: Yeah, probably, or else they're just being hidden in one of those barns or something and having the hell scared out of them. But I would not be surprised if they'd been murdered, Mr. President. Pretty tough characters.
>
> LBJ: How old are the kids?
>
> NK: Twenty and twenty-four and twenty-two.

At 4:05 P.M. on June 23, J. Edgar Hoover called the president to inform him that the trio's burned car had been found on the Choctaw reservation.

JEH: Apparently what's happened — these men have been killed.

LBJ: Now what would make you think they've been killed?

JEH: Because it is the same car they were in in Philadelphia, Mississippi. This is merely an assumption that probably they were burned in the car. On the other hand, they may have been taken out and killed on the outside.

LBJ: Or maybe kidnapped and locked up.

JEH: I would doubt whether those people down there would give them even that much of a break.

Although Hoover and McCormack advised Johnson against meeting with the families of the missing young men, after finding out about the burned car, the president decided to meet with or telephone the families. He called Lee White and said, "Tell 'em what-all we've done and let me come over and say a word. And I just ought to tell 'em we've found the car. I'd have to tell 'em." White's response: "That's gonna be tough."

When Attorney General Robert Kennedy was informed by Doar that the young men were missing, he ordered Joseph Sullivan, a senior FBI investigator at that time working in New Orleans, to get to Mississippi to find out what had happened. As soon as the charred car was discovered, almost 400 sailors from the Meridian Naval Air Station, scores of FBI agents (ultimately 258 FBI agents worked on the case), and other federal employees began searching the Bogue Chitto Swamp and other areas surrounding the town of Philadelphia for the bodies of the three men. This FBI assignment was not a plum one. Mississippi is brutally hot and humid in the summer, and the locals did not like federal officers intruding into the lives of Mississippians.

In 1974, John Doar testified before the U.S. Senate Judiciary Committee, Subcommittee on Constitutional Rights. His remarks, entitled "The Performance of the FBI in Investigating Violations of Federal Laws Protecting the Right to Vote, 1960–1967," criticized Hoover's and the FBI's actions in this area of civil rights: "Many FBI agents resigned rather than go to Mississippi." Those who went ran smack into Hoover's disdainful views of the civil rights protesters and, consequently, were not able to overcome "the Bureau's prior performance, its deference to the rule of white over black and its indifference to the Rule of Law."

Hoover's attitude about these civil rights volunteers was well known even in the 1960s. At a press conference in Washington, D.C., on November 18, 1964, he declared, "I have been one of those states' righters all my life." He maintained that the FBI lacked the authority to protect anyone from local violence and intimidation — and he opposed any legislation giving the FBI such powers. The FBI would not protect "everybody who goes down to try to reform or re-educate the Negro population in the South."

In addition to Hoover's attitude and behavior regarding the civil rights movement leaders, the DOJ policy with respect to a massive invasion by federal agents into southern states was one that respected the principle of federalism more than it did the protection of civil rights workers from vicious southern racist attacks on them, including beating, shootings, and killings. In a mid-July 1964 letter, Burke Marshall wrote Neil Staebler, a DOJ staff lawyer, that "problems of protection had to be the responsibility of local law enforcement agencies." All federal agents could do was to try to "induce" these agency personnel to meet their obligations. Failing that, he wrote, the last step would be for federal courts to order law enforcement officers to protect persons threatened by violence.

Because of federal noninvolvement in policing the South, in Mississippi and Alabama it was "not a punishable crime to kill a Negro or a civil rights worker." For civil rights leaders, on the other hand, the failure of the DOJ to do more to prevent violence and murder by segregationists was, as civil rights leader Willy Branton (of the Voter Education Project) said, "one of the great failures on the part of the DOJ."

Thurgood Marshall, soon to be the U.S. solicitor general, responded with anguish to the news reports of the disappearance and then the killing of the three young men: "It hurt. Two Jewish kids and one black one get their lives snuffed out by racists. As a [federal court of] appeals judge I couldn't say publicly how angry I was. When I read that a police car had taken the kids to the deserted area where they were murdered, I couldn't eat, drink, or do anything."

One year later, as solicitor general, Marshall could do something;

he was the government's spokesperson when the case of *U.S. v. Price* was argued in the Supreme Court during its 1965 term.

———

For more than forty days — many were eleven-hour days in sweltering, humid heat reaching into the three-digit zone — federal forces scoured the area around the swamp. Troopers from the Mississippi State Highway Patrol accompanied these federal searchers. However, they were not there to assist in the search; their mission, announced by Governor Paul Johnson, was to "be certain that the people's houses and property of this area are protected at all times."

On July 10, Hoover reluctantly established an FBI office in Jackson, Mississippi, which instantly became the largest FBI operation outside Washington, D.C. More than 150 FBI agents, with Ray Moore as the Special Agent in Charge (SAC), were initially assigned to the state to hunt for the three men and, belatedly, to "show the colors."

Rewards, as much as $50,000, were announced in the hope that someone in the area would break the conspiracy of silence and provide the federal agents with information about the whereabouts of Schwerner and the others. After more than a month, John Doar said that "Neshoba County remained silent; only *extraordinary methods* and a maximum effort by the FBI" could bring the killers to justice (my emphasis).

No one claimed the reward, and, it is alleged by some, the FBI evidently had to resort to an ingenious, top secret — and illegal — plan, an "extraordinary method," to finally uncover the bodies of the civil rights workers.

———

A KKK Informant Is "Coerced," and the Bodies Are Discovered

July ended without the FBI getting any closer to discovering the whereabouts of the three young men. Nothing had worked for the federal investigators. They had questioned more than 1,000 Mississippians, including 500 Klansmen, and still had not located the trio. The conspiracy of silence on the part of the Klansmen and other whites living in Neshoba County was extremely effective.

Rewards had been posted for information about the fate of the three civil rights workers. No one came forward with information in return for the reward money. The FBI's informants in the Klan were of no help at all. "The FBI was very embarrassed," said a high government source to Jerry Capeci, a reporter for the *New York Daily News*, in 1994. According to Capeci and, in 1998, Bill Moushey, an investigative reporter for the *Pittsburgh Post-Gazette*, an unbelievably unconventional and illegal action was taken — ordered by J. Edgar Hoover — to find the bodies of the civil rights workers.

The conventional story of how the FBI discovered the bodies is familiar to many. On the night of July 31–August 1, 1964, after searching vainly for the bodies for a month and a half, the FBI was told by a paid KKK informant, thereafter placed under the protection of the federal government, of the location of the three men's graves: on the farm of wealthy Klansman Olen Burrage, six miles southwest of Philadelphia. The informant was paid $30,000 for the information. Three days later, on August 4, 1964, the bodies were discovered, buried ten to seventeen feet below the crest of an earthen dam a few miles southwest of Philadelphia off Highway 21.

In his book *Pillar of Fire*, Taylor Branch recounted the event. Chief Inspector Sullivan's FBI agents spread many rumors about the upcoming break in the case of the three missing civil rights workers. Sullivan's contrived "rumor blitz" was designed not to stimulate the flow of information but to conceal the identity of the one informant who had already talked. For $30,000, contingent upon positive identification, Sullivan had just bought precise information that the three bodies lay beneath a fresh earthen dam on the Olen Burrage farm.

At about the time the rumors were flying in Neshoba County, others were flying in the hallways of the FBI headquarters in Washington, D.C. Sullivan had returned to Washington, and there was speculation that there was going to be a major break in the case. According to Branch, "There was admiring talk of nighttime FBI raids to shove condom-wrapped shotgun shells into the rectums of hostile Klansmen, daring them to complain, and of Mafia informants secretly imported to extract information by old-fashioned torture."

The other version of how the FBI located the bodies is straight out of a wide-screen gangster epic playing at a cineplex. It is the one alluded to by Branch and others but rejected by most persons who have examined the strange events surrounding the discovery of the bodies. Although former FBI agents involved in the Mississippi investigation — including Sullivan — insist that the story is "totally inaccurate," others who knew about the incident state simply, "It happened. Everybody's going to say, 'Nah, it never happened,' but it did."

Hoover was under intense pressure — from the president, the families of the missing men, civil rights organizations, and the media — to find the bodies. Having absolutely no lucky breaks, he ordered his New York office to send a Mafioso killer, Gregory Scarpa Sr., alias "The Grim Reaper," a member of the Joseph Columbo crime family, down South to assist the FBI in forcing information from a Klansman. At the time, Scarpa was an FBI tipster in New York working with his FBI control agent, Anthony Vilano. He considered himself a patriot; according to Vilano, "He was a cowboy. He was an action guy."

After agreeing to cooperate with the FBI, Scarpa and his girlfriend flew down to Miami, Florida, and checked in at a major hotel to establish an alibi. He then flew alone to New Orleans, where he met two of his New York FBI handlers. The trio drove to Philadelphia, Mississippi, where FBI agents who had been working in Mississippi since the June disappearance pointed out to Scarpa a local merchant who was a member of the Neshoba County Klavern.

Scarpa entered the store and purchased a television set. He told the merchant he would return at closing to pick it up. When he returned, Scarpa asked him to help him load the television into the car's trunk. Outside, Scarpa hit the merchant over the head, threw the unconscious man into the trunk of the car, and drove off to a prearranged location. He brought the kidnapped merchant into the house.

There Scarpa tied the frightened man to a chair and demanded to know "what happened to the three kids." After being beaten for almost three days, the merchant gave Scarpa information. Scarpa then went outside and spoke to the local FBI agents, who told him the story was phony. Scarpa went back in and continued to beat the merchant. A second version was also labeled false by the FBI agents. At that point, Scarpa asked for and was given a gun, and he went into the house again. He stuck the gun barrel into the merchant's mouth and demanded, "Tell me the fucking truth or I'll blow your fucking brains out." Terrified, the man gave Scarpa the location of the graves and the names of those who had participated in the planning and execution of the murders of Schwerner, Goodman, and Chaney. Scarpa returned to New York City, where he continued in his role as mobster and FBI informant until he died in federal prison in June 1994.

The identity of the person who gave the FBI the location of the dead civil rights workers remains a mystery to this day. Known only as "Mr. X," that person's identity, known only by the FBI's chief inspector, remains locked in Sullivan's head. In 1989 he said to a *Jackson Clarion-Ledger* reporter, "I'm still not talking about Mr. X." Sullivan did, however, say that there was never a $30,000 payoff or any amount of money paid to the unnamed informant. "*Nobody transmitted money* for information on the bodies. I don't know anything about anybody being paid any money" (my emphasis).

The information — from whatever source — proved to be correct, and a few days later, on August 4, 1964, the FBI announced that the bodies of the three missing men had been recovered. An August 16 FBI report described the recovery of the bodies. Heavy earthmoving equipment was brought from Jackson to the "Old Jolly farm," the property of Olen Burrage, located on a dirt access road west of Highway 21, about six miles southwest of Philadelphia, and the excavation began at 8:00 A.M. According to the report:

> At approximately 2:50 P.M., the pungent odor of decaying flesh was clearly discernible [from the pit dug by the machines]. . . . At 3:18 the outline of a human body appeared and . . . approximately 2 hours later Body #1 [Michael Schwerner] . . . was uncovered. . . . At 5:07 the body of a second individual [Andrew Goodman] . . . was located, partially under Body #1. . . . At 5:14 P.M. the remains of a third body [James Chaney] was unearthed. . . . It is estimated that approximately 27,000 cubic feet of earth was removed in the exhumation of these three bodies.

Three hours later, the Neshoba County coroner, accompanied by Deputy Sheriff Price, arrived. After the coroner's examination was completed, the bodies were placed in large plastic body bags and sealed for transportation to the University of Mississippi Medical Center in Jackson. The hearse carrying the three bodies departed the burial site at 11:14 P.M. for the two-hour ride to Jackson.

Reviewing the correspondence between Nicholas Katzenbach, the deputy U.S. attorney general, and Al Rosen, the assistant director of the FBI, one cannot be sure of which version of how the FBI received the information to believe. Katzenbach was working with Burke Marshall and John Doar on preparing information to present to a federal grand jury in Biloxi, Mississippi, in late September 1964. They were seeking to indict almost two dozen Klansmen for violating the civil rights of the dead men, and Marshall had an important question for the FBI. In a September 16 memo to his FBI colleague, Mr. Belmont, Rosen wrote:

> [Katzenbach] then brought up a question which has previously been raised by Burke Marshall. It is recalled that Marshall stated in connection with the finding of the bodies of the three civil rights workers by the FBI [that] *it is just incredible* as to how the Agents were able to find the boys in the location they did based solely on an intensive search. (my emphasis)

Basically the two DOJ men wanted to know if the FBI had information not divulged to them or "whether any of our evidence is tainted. [We] ought to be aware of the facts," said Katzenbach, "so that [we] would not be caught by surprise [by the defense attorneys] or take action which was undesirable." Rosen assured Katzenbach that no information was withheld from the DOJ. However, in the memo to Belmont, Rosen wrote: "The Director [Hoover] believes that the Bureau under no circumstances should disclose information which we must retain in full and complete confidence [about how the bureau located the bodies]."

A few days later, on September 21, 1964, another memo was sent from Rosen to Belmont informing him of the latest conversation between Rosen and Katzenbach. Evidently the DOJ knew there was an informant and wanted the name of the person who told the FBI where the bodies were located. Rosen wrote, "I told him I could not identify the source of our information, that if we did the source would immediately be killed; . . . and that it did not appear essential . . . that the source be identified."

These meetings, telephone calls, and memos suggest that the FBI leadership needed to keep an absolutely tight lid on the informant's identity. More disconcerting to the DOJ lawyers preparing to present evidence to the federal grand jury was the "incredible luck" of the FBI agents in miraculously discovering the three bodies, corpses buried under more than 150 tons of red clay dam. How was it possible, given the highly successful conspiracy of silence in Neshoba and Lauderdale Counties, to get that informant to reveal the location of the bodies and the names of the Klansmen who participated in the executions? The FBI did have something to hide; requests for information about Scarpa's role, if any, in the discovery of the bodies were made under the Freedom of Information Act (FOIA). They were fruitless efforts.

The bodies had been found. The next step was to determine who was involved in the killing and to then figure out where they would be prosecuted. Once the perpetrators were identified, would they be tried for murder in a Mississippi court, with Mississippians sitting on the jury and wielding the gavel, with Mississippians prosecuting and defending the accused? In the history of the state's criminal justice system, no white Mississippian had ever been convicted of murdering blacks or civil rights workers.

Or would they be tried in federal district court in Mississippi? The federal criminal code did not punish the crime of murder; thus, if the trial were to take place in federal court, the accused would face much less severe punishment if found guilty of conspiracy to take the lives of the three young men without providing them with "due process of law" in violation of the Fourteenth Amendment.

CHAPTER 4

Informants and Indictments

There are three sovereignties involved [in the killings]. There's the United States
government, the state of Mississippi, and there's J. Edgar Hoover.
LYNDON BAINES JOHNSON, JUNE 1964

When the FBI investigation, code-named "MIBURN" (for "Mississippi Burning"), into the disappearance and then the murders of
Schwerner, Chaney, and Goodman ended, there were 150,000 pages
of data in the file. By June 1964, the FBI had successfully infiltrated
many of the Mississippi Klaverns. After the late June disappearance
of the trio, Joseph Sullivan was chosen to serve as the FBI's Major
Case Inspector. For nine months, June 1964 through March 1965,
Sullivan, working out of Meridian, Mississippi, managed the FBI's
investigation until MIBURN ended.

It was a very difficult assignment for Sullivan and the FBI agents
working with him in the state. As already noted, rather than work in
Mississippi, some FBI personnel chose to resign. Those who worked
in the state felt the bitter hatred of the segregationists and experienced
the same wall of silence on the part of the great number of white Mississippians who chose that route to avoid danger to themselves and
their families.

The federal authorities not only faced the silence of the majority;
they also faced — as did the civil rights workers in the state — the
intense loathing of the state's local law enforcement officers. From the
first moments the FBI agents entered the picture, there was a palpable
enmity directed at the federal law enforcement officers by most of the
state's police and law enforcement personnel. Unfortunately, this feeling extended to those men and women responsible for the operation
of the state's criminal justice system — including prosecutors, judges,
and jurors.

The Enmity and Distrust between Federal and State Law Enforcement Officers

For Sullivan, as for so many others, Philadelphia Klansmen and their neighbors were tight-lipped and unwilling to do anything to help the FBI. "They [the KKK] owned the place," he said. "In spirit everyone belonged to the Klan." Local Neshoba County residents repeatedly sent FBI agents on "wild goose chases," Sullivan recalled. The two men who confessed to the FBI in the fall of 1964, Jim Jordan and Horace D. Barnette, were Lauderdale County Klansmen. Sullivan said that "if the Neshoba Klavern carried out the murders on their own, they would almost certainly have gotten away with it."

This "silence" reality faced by Sullivan and his special agents working in the state spiraled downward for them. As days went by with no breakthroughs, Sullivan experienced, as he said later, "the pressure from Washington for some solution. . . . It was really intense." Sullivan had to travel frequently to Jackson to meet with agitated officials from Washington, D.C., including the FBI's assistant director, Al Rosen, the director, J. Edgar Hoover himself, as well as Burke Marshall and John Doar from the Department of Justice.

Hundreds of FBI Special Agents interviewed thousands of persons about the events of June 21 and 22, 1964. Most of the raw and finished reports filed by the agents are still unavailable even under the Freedom of Information Act. (The FOIA's guidelines provide at least seven categories of information whose secrecy can be maintained by a federal agency. This enables an agency to refuse to provide requested documentation.) Furthermore, the documents that have been released have a great many blackouts — Magic Marker sweeps across data on the documents the agency does not feel bound to release.

The FBI, under orders from J. Edgar Hoover, even denied federal prosecutors information the Department of Justice felt was important in preparing its case for federal grand juries and in responding to objections and filings by defense attorneys in the effort to bring the killers to some kind of justice. In addition, Hoover refused to allow any FBI agents to testify in scheduled state grand jury proceedings planned for Neshoba County in September and October 1964. He also ordered the agency not to release any data in the MIBURN file when the state attorney general asked for the documents in order to file murder charges against the Klansmen.

The reasoning of the federal government was understandable: "We could not trust the State to do the right thing with the information; indeed, the wrong thing might be done to prospective witnesses for the prosecution in the federal cases." As a consequence, the state did not bring charges against any Mississippian in 1964 for the murders of the three young men. (No charges have been brought against the killers of Schwerner, Chaney, and Goodman in the forty years since they were executed.)

Sullivan's investigation was, almost from the beginning, broadened to include the many complaints of local police brutality against civil rights workers that occurred between the end of June and the middle of August 1964, when the Mississippi Freedom Summer project officially ended. Furthermore, the FBI had to investigate the large number of Mississippi churches destroyed or damaged during this period. Between June 15 and September 20, 1964, a total of thirty-one places of worship — or the homes of the clergymen — were firebombed in the night. Examples, taken from a COFO report, include the following incidents:

June 15— Hattiesburg, Mississippi. Rosary Roman Catholic Church; Pastor: Father John Kerston. Auditorium gutted by fire after a meeting during which the pastor said the following words: "These Negroes were discussing means of averting racial violence."

June 21— Brandon, Rankin County, Mississippi. Sweet Rest Church of Christ Holiness; Pastor: Reverend L. C. Robbins. Molotov cocktail. Fire started: damage not extensive (This church was subsequently destroyed in early August.)

August 11— Gluckstadt, Mississippi (near Clinton), Mount Pleasant Church; Pastor: Rev. N. O. Taylor. The church was severely damaged by fire. It was being used as a Freedom School.

September 16— Valley View, Mississippi (Madison County, 8 miles from Canton.) Saint John the Baptist Church. The church burned to the ground between 11:00 and midnight. This church was the first ever used in rural Madison County for voter registration, and it was the location of the CORE Freedom School this past summer.

By the time the MIBURN investigation ended, in the spring of 1965, Inspector Sullivan looked forward to moving back to the Washington, D.C., area. It had been a grueling, nearly yearlong investigation into the actions of an organization, the Klan, he thoroughly despised. What angered him most, however, was the fact that a great many of Mississippi's eighty-two county sheriff's offices were also the homes of known — and respected — Klansmen. At times Sullivan completely lost his temper and angrily tongue-lashed the Klansmen in sheriff's clothing.

According to a Sovereignty Commission report filed by Hopkins on September 9, 1964, in one such event Sullivan verbally attacked law enforcement officers in Neshoba County. An FBI agent who had been threatened by a Klansman in Philadelphia called Sullivan to seek permission to make a federal arrest. Instead, Sullivan drove from Meridian to the town and called Price and a policeman to the FBI headquarters in Philadelphia, located in the Delphia Hotel. According to the report, Sullivan

> chewed them out worse than he [Price] had ever been chewed out in the army. He allegedly stated to Price that if he didn't intend to enforce the local laws that he, Sullivan, had men that would enforce them. He stated, according to Price, that if they did not intend to enforce the laws that they should turn in their badges. [After arguing about the incident involving the threat against the FBI agent earlier that day], Inspector Sullivan completely lost his temper, cursed, threatened and became highly agitated and made unreasonable demands on the local [police] officials. . . . This incident is reported to show that there is a possibility of serious trouble between city, county, and federal officials in Neshoba County.

This animosity between the federal investigators and county and local law enforcement officers existed from the first moments the FBI agents began searching for Schwerner, Chaney, and Goodman. For one thing, the FBI investigators had information that a great many of these law enforcement officers were Klansmen who had no problem engaging in church burnings, beating up civil rights workers, and, in the case of Schwerner, Chaney, and Goodman, committing cold-blooded murders of persons who came to Mississippi to challenge the status quo of racism in the state. This categorical mistrust, on the part of all law enforcement agencies working in the state that summer, carried over into prosecutorial decisions by the FBI, the federal government lawyers, and state and county prosecutors and judges.

The Problematic Matter of Jurisdiction

The bodies had been found, and some information had been acquired about who the criminals were. The next question was, Who had jurisdiction, and thus where would a trial take place? At that time, Mississippi had never convicted a white person of killing a black person or a civil rights worker. Indeed, on most occasions in the past, there had never even been an indictment.

On the other hand, in 1964, the federal criminal code did not provide the DOJ with an opportunity to indict the Klansmen on murder charges. If the federal government was to indict and try the men who killed the civil rights workers, it had to be a proceeding involving the lesser charge of conspiring to deprive the three young men of their federally protected rights without due process of law.

In September, both the DOJ lawyers and the Neshoba County district attorney began preparing for the convening of grand juries in their respective jurisdictions. The federal government was set to convene a federal grand jury panel in the federal courthouse in Biloxi, on the Mississippi Gulf coast. The DOJ was preparing a case against a number of Klansmen from Lauderdale and Neshoba Counties who, the federal lawyers believed, were involved in the firebombing of the Mount Zion Methodist Church and the murders of the three civil rights workers.

The DOJ lawyers had found a number of black victims of the beatings and church burning and had subpoenaed them to speak before the grand jury. They prepared to present additional information about the conspiracy to a federal grand jury sitting in Biloxi. At the same time, a Neshoba County judge began to issue subpoenas to the FBI Special Agents who were working on the MIBURN investigation. This set off legal clashes between federal lawyers and the FBI and

Mississippi judges and prosecutors that quickly escalated into a major battle between Mississippi and the federal government.

By mid-September, the DOJ, with Departmental Attorney David R. Owen in charge and working out of the Meridian office, prepared subpoenas to issue to 100 individuals "in connection with the foregoing grand jury hearing concerning the MIBURN case." The grand jury was set to commence its work on September 21, 1964. Owen was hard at work preparing the criminal charges, based on 18 *United States Code (U.S.C.)* Sections 241 and 242, against the Klansmen.

After receiving a report from Owen, Hoover sent a letter to Walter Jenkins, President Johnson's Special Assistant, on September 18, 1964. Hoover informed him that the information collected by Owen, including victims' testimony, "will be presented to a Federal Grand Jury at Biloxi, Mississippi commencing September 21, 1964. The wealth of information concerning numerous possible violations of Civil Rights statutes as reflected in our extensive reports covering approximately 3,278 pages will be presented for the Grand Jury's consideration. To date, approximately 100 witnesses have been subpoenaed to appear before the Grand Jury."

At the same time, however, Neshoba County Circuit Judge O. H. Barnett (a cousin of former Mississippi governor Ross Barnett) signed subpoenas that called for nine FBI Special Agents — all working on the investigating team studying the murders of the trio of civil rights men — to appear before a state grand jury investigating the same incident. Federal officials, in both the DOJ and the FBI, categorically refused to allow any of the data collected in the MIBURN investigation to be released to anyone in Mississippi. They certainly did not want FBI agents forced to testify under oath about the information gathered by the bureau.

Newly appointed Acting Attorney General Katzenbach (Bobby Kennedy had stepped down during the summer of 1964) told the FBI SAC in Jackson, Mississippi — and J. Edgar Hoover — that "disclosure at this time to persons other than the federal grand jury would be inimical to the public interest and would seriously burden and impede the DOJ in effectively discharging its lawful responsibilities in the administration of the criminal laws of the United States."

By September 24, Hoover telegraphed Judge Barnett informing him that the FBI agents will be unable to testify before the state grand jury at this time regarding the death of the three civil rights workers, as they have been instructed . . . not to disclose before that grand jury any information relating to material or information contained in the files of the DOJ, or any information obtained in connection with any official DOJ investigation. In the circumstances, I assume the agents will be excused from appearing before the grand jury Monday.

On Sunday, the day before the state grand jury was scheduled to commence its work, federal officials met with the judge and the Neshoba County prosecutor, Raiford Jones. They handed them a note signed by Hoover, which said, "When the federal proceedings are completed and at such time when it does not conflict with our federal obligation, we will fully cooperate with state and local authorities in making available such evidence and testimony as we possess pertaining to violations of local law."

The DOJ did not know how the judge would respond and, even before the Sunday meeting, had contingency plans worked out in case the judge ordered the FBI agents to appear before the grand jury. If ordered to appear, they would do so but would refuse to testify about MIBURN work. If they were brought before Judge Barnett

> they will maintain the same position and cite the Departmental instructions. If the Judge rules the Agents to be in contempt and levies a fine, the imposition of the fine will immediately be appealed. If the Judge . . . asks that they be detained in jail, the DOJ attorney will immediately file papers to obtain a writ of habeas corpus from Federal Judge Sidney Mize of the U.S. District Court sitting in Biloxi to have the agents released.

The solution evolved at the very last moment. Burke Marshall suggested that a DOJ representative appear before the Neshoba County grand jurors and present the federal government's position. The clash ended quietly because of Marshall's penchant for negotiating and settling without creating a federal-state crisis.

However, the initial federal effort to bring charges against Klansmen known to be involved in the beatings, church burning, and murder of the trio, did not succeed. The federal attorneys were not sanguine about the possibility of getting an indictment. The FBI's assistant director, Rosen, told Hoover that "the grand jury had been selected without any input from the DOJ lawyers; they did not know the attitude of the jurors. [Burke Marshall] said that some of them, of course, were resistant and had the attitude that you couldn't believe anything that a Negro said."

The grand jury consisted of twenty-two white persons and one black. It failed to hand down indictments against the defendants (more than twenty of them) by a margin of one vote. Twelve votes were needed to indict; evidently there were eleven who voted to indict. With the failure, the DOJ went back to square one and began preparations for presenting evidence to another federal grand jury.

However, the quarrel between federal and state authorities did not end. In early December 1964, a meeting was held in Governor Paul Johnson's home in Jackson, Mississippi. In attendance were FBI agents, the state attorney general, the commissioner of public safety, and the county attorney of Neshoba County. The federal agents informed the state leaders that the FBI had two confessions from Klansmen involved in the murders. They were "ready to make arrests for violations of federal law, although they did not state the names of the persons to be arrested," wrote W. H. Johnson Jr., a lawyer in the state attorney general's office, to the executive director of the Sovereignty Commission, Erle Johnson Jr.

> They requested that we make arrests on the state level of the same individuals that they planned to arrest and charge these individuals with murder. We informed [the agents] that we would not be able to make arrests for murder unless we could see the written confessions and to know firsthand what the evidence would be. . . . We were refused the opportunity to see the written confessions, to talk with the individuals who allegedly had confessed, and to see any other evidence.

The FBI then informed the state prosecutors that the "federal government had decided to go ahead with the arrests on the federal level and charge the accused individuals with violations of federal law based on an old civil rights statute (conspiracy). . . . The State," concluded Johnson's letter, "has not refused to prosecute this case, but of course must have sufficient evidence to present in order to obtain indictments and to try those charged with the crime." To this day, Mississippi prosecutors have never charged any of the alleged killers with the murders of the civil rights trio.

———

Using an 1870 Federal Criminal Conspiracy Statute against the Klan

All the Department of Justice's indictments argued that the Klansmen acted in violation of 18 *U.S.C.*, Sections 241 and 242. In its entirety, Section 242 first came into the law as Section 2 of the 1866 Civil Rights Act. After passage of the Fourteenth Amendment in 1868, it was reenacted and amended as Section 17 of the Enforcement Act of 1870. In addition, Section 6 was enacted in the 1870 legislation. Amended in the intervening decades, in 1874, 1909, 1948, and 1996, old Sections 6 and 17 of the 1870 Enforcement Act are now Sections 241 and 242 of 18 *U.S.C.* They read as follows:

Section 241— Conspiracy against rights
If two or more persons conspire to injure, oppress, threaten, or intimidate any person in any State, Territory, Commonwealth, Possession, or District in the free exercise or enjoyment of any right or privilege secured to him by the Constitution or laws of the United States, or because of his having so exercised the same; or if two or more persons go in disguise on the highway, or on the premises of another, with intent to prevent or hinder his free exercise or enjoyment of any right or privilege so secured: They shall be fined not more than $5,000 under this title or imprisoned not more than ten years, or both.

Section 242— Deprivation of rights under color of law (Misdemeanor)
Whoever, under color of any law, statute, ordinance, regulation, or custom, willfully subjects any person in any State, Territory, Commonwealth, Possession, or District to the deprivation of any rights, privileges, or immunities secured or protected by the Constitution or laws of the United States, or to different punishments, pains, or penalties, on account of such person being an alien, or by reason of his color, or race, than are prescribed for the punishment of citizens, shall be fined not more than $1,000 or imprisoned not more than one year, or both.

In an important 1876 case, *U.S. v. Cruikshank*, a unanimous U.S. Supreme Court severely restricted use of the Enforcement Act by the Department of Justice. The case began with the 1872 state election results in Louisiana, which were disputed between the regular Republicans and a coalition of liberal Republicans and Democrats, with each side inaugurating its own governor and legislature. A federal district judge ruled that the regular Republicans were the victors, and newly reelected President Ulysses S. Grant sent federal troops to ensure compliance with the judicial decree. Many whites in Louisiana refused to accept that decision. They established a shadow government and used paramilitary units known as the White League to intimidate and attack blacks and white Republicans.

The worst incident of violence was the Colfax Massacre of April 13, 1873. The fighting left two white men and almost 100 black men dead, with half of the latter killed after they surrendered. Federal officials arrested and indicted more than 100 white men, including their leader, William Cruikshank, for violating Section 6 (now Section 241) of the 1870 Enforcement Act. They were later freed, however, when the U.S. Supreme Court ruled that the basis for their prosecution was unconstitutional: the indictments did not specifically allege the denial of federal rights protected by the Constitution. Chief Justice Morrison R. Waite, for the Court, stated:

> The counts of an indictment which, in general language, charge the defendants with an intent to hinder and prevent citizens of the United States, of African descent, therein named, in the free exercise and enjoyment of the rights, privileges, immunities, and protection, granted and secured to them respectively as citizens of the United States, and of the State of Louisiana, because they were persons of African descent, and with the intent to hinder and prevent them in the several and free exercise and enjoyment of every, each, all, and singular the several rights and privileges granted and secured to them by the constitution and laws of the United States, do not specify any particular right the enjoyment of which the conspirators intended to hinder or prevent, are too vague and general, lack the certainty and precision required by the established rule of criminal pleading, and are therefore not good and sufficient in law.

Cruikshank became a watershed event in the federal government's retreat from the policies and principles of the Radical Reconstruction Congress (1865–1878). Its precedent remained the law of the land for almost seven decades — until the NAACP, under Thurgood Marshall's astute leadership, encouraged the lawyers in the newly created Civil Rights Division in the DOJ to restore the teeth in Sections 241 and 242.

In the 1940s (in *Screws v. United States* [1945]), in the 1950s, in two cases involving the same event and raising key questions regarding Sections 241 and 242, respectively (*U.S. v. Williams* [1951; known as *Williams* I] and *Williams v. U.S.* [1951; known as *Williams* II]), and again in the 1960s (in *Monroe v. Pape* [1961], *U.S. v. Price*, and *U.S. v. Guest*), new U.S. Supreme Court majorities found ways to reenergize Sections 241 and 242 of the long-dormant 1870 legislation. In *Screws*, Claude Screws, the sheriff of Baker County, Georgia, arrested a black man for stealing a tire. The man was then brutally beaten by Screws while handcuffed and died soon afterward. Screws was charged with violating Section 20 (now Section 242) of 18 *U.S.C.* for violating the dead man's federal due process rights "under color of law." Screws's lawyers argued that the conviction was unconstitutional, presenting the Court's reasoning in *Cruikshank*.

A slim Court majority, however, concluded that the challenged statute was valid, although the case was remanded because the trial judge had not given the jurors the proper definition of the phrase "willfully," and the justices did not examine the question of intent on the part of the sheriff. "We are of the view," wrote Associate Justice William O. Douglas in the judgment of the Court,

> that if Section 20 is confined more narrowly than the lower courts confined it, it can be preserved as one of the sanctions to the great rights which the Fourteenth Amendment was designed to secure. . . . We repeat that the presence of a bad purpose or evil intent alone may not be sufficient. We do say that a requirement of a specific intent to deprive a person of a federal right by decision or other rule of law saves the section from any charge of unconstitutionality on the grounds of vagueness.

The *Williams* cases were the first ones heard by the U.S. Supreme Court that "squarely confronted the point at issue in the *Price* litigation." The Court sustained dismissal of an indictment under Section

241, but it did not, as federal trial judge Cox "incorrectly assumed" in his 1965 order, hold that Section 241 was inapplicable to Fourteenth Amendment rights.

In 1947 a Florida corporation employed a detective agency to investigate thefts of its property. The inquiry was conducted by Williams, the head of the agency, and among the participants were two of his employees and a member of the Miami police force detailed to assist in the investigation. Certain of the company's employees fell under suspicion. Williams and his collaborators, without arresting the suspects, took them one by one to a shack on the company's premises. There the investigators subjected the suspects to the familiar "third degree," which, after blows, kicks, threats, and prolonged exposure to a brilliant light, yielded "confessions."

Williams and the other three were thereupon indicted for violation of 18 *U.S.C.* 241 and 242. Williams was convicted under 242, the indictment alleging that he "willfully, under color of the laws, statutes, ordinances, regulations and customs of the State of Florida, . . . subjected . . . an inhabitant of the State of Florida, to deprivation of the rights, privileges and immunities secured to him and protected by the Fourteenth Amendment." The other defendants were acquitted of the charges under 242, and as to all defendants a mistrial was declared under 241.

This outcome of the indictment under 241 and 242 was followed by a new indictment against the four defendants under 241, which alleged that "acting under the laws of the State of Florida," the defendants "conspired to injure . . . a citizen of the United States and of the State of Florida, in the free exercise and enjoyment of the rights and privileges secured to him and protected by the Fourteenth Amendment." This time all the defendants were convicted, but on appeal the U.S. Court of Appeals for the Fifth Circuit reversed. It held that in the conspiracy provision of 241 "the Congress had in mind the federal rights and privileges which appertain to citizens as such and not the general rights extended to all persons by the clause of the Fourteenth Amendment." In the alternative, the court concluded that a broader construction of 241 would render it void for indefiniteness, and that "there was error in the judge's charge as well as in the exclusion of evidence of the prior acquittal of three of the defendants. . . .

We brought the case here because important questions in the administration of civil rights legislation are raised."

The U.S. Supreme Court split 4:4:1 on the merits when the case came to the justices on appeal. Four justices, in an opinion written by Felix Frankfurter, maintained that 241 "only covers conduct which interferes with rights arising from the substantive powers of the Federal government." Four other justices, in an opinion written by Justice Douglas, read 241 very differently: "The statute plainly cover[s] conspiracies to injure others in the exercise of their Fourteenth Amendment rights." Dismissal of the indictment was affirmed because the ninth justice, Hugo L. Black, voted with those who joined Frankfurter, but "for an entirely different reason — that the prosecution was barred by *res judicata* — and [he expressed no view] on the [issue] of 241." Given the 4:4:1 vote breakdown in *Williams* I, the question of the "proper construction of 241" remained open until the 1960s — and the decision of the U.S. Supreme Court in *U.S. v. Price.*

In *Monroe v. Pape*, which was, on point of law, a civil suit for damages under Section 1983 of the *U.S.C.*, the U.S. Supreme Court, in an opinion authored by Justice Douglas, did have cause to examine the scope of Section 241. The complaint

> alleged that 13 Chicago police officers broke into petitioners' home in the early morning, routed them from bed, made them stand naked in the living room, and ransacked every room, emptying drawers and ripping mattress covers. It further alleges that Mr. Monroe was then taken to the police station and detained on "open" charges for 10 hours, while he was interrogated about a two-day-old murder, that he was not taken before a magistrate, though one was accessible, that he was not permitted to call his family or attorney, that he was subsequently released without criminal charges being preferred against him. It is alleged that the officers had no search warrant and no arrest warrant, and that they acted "under color of the statutes, ordinances, regulations, customs and usages" of Illinois and of the City of Chicago.
>
> The City of Chicago moved to dismiss the complaint on the ground that it is not liable under the Civil Rights Acts nor for acts committed in performance of its governmental functions. All defen-

dants moved to dismiss, alleging that the complaint alleged no cause of action under those Acts or under the Federal Constitution. The District Court dismissed the complaint. The Court of Appeals affirmed, relying on its earlier decision, *Stift v. Lynch*. The case is here on a writ of certiorari which we granted because of a seeming conflict of that ruling with our prior cases.

Petitioners claim that the invasion of their home and the subsequent search without a warrant and the arrest and detention of Mr. Monroe without a warrant and without arraignment constituted a deprivation of their "rights, privileges, or immunities secured by the Constitution." . . . It has been said that, when 18 *U.S.C.* 241 made criminal a conspiracy "to injure, oppress, threaten, or intimidate any citizen in the free exercise or enjoyment of any right or privilege secured to him by the Constitution," it embraced only rights that an individual has by reason of his relation to the central government, not to state governments. *United States v. Williams,* 341 U.S. 70. Cf. *United States v. Cruikshank,* 92 U.S. 542; *Ex parte Yarbrough,* 110 U.S. 651; *Guinn v. United States,* 238 U.S. 347. But the history of the section of the Civil Rights Act presently involved does not permit such a narrow interpretation.

Justice Douglas concluded: "It is abundantly clear that one reason the legislation was passed was to afford a federal right in federal courts because, by reason of prejudice, passion, neglect, intolerance or otherwise, state laws might not be enforced and the claims of citizens to the enjoyment of rights, privileges, and immunities guaranteed by the Fourteenth Amendment might be denied by the state agencies."

In *Price*'s companion case, *United States v. Guest,* Justice Potter Stewart, writing for the U.S. Supreme Court, said, "When 241 speaks of 'any right or privilege secured . . . by the Constitution or laws of the United States,' it means precisely that. . . . Since the gravamen of the offense is conspiracy, the requirement that the offender must act with a specific intent to interfere with the federal rights in question is satisfied."

By the mid-1960s, then, the U.S. Supreme Court majority, under the leadership of Chief Justice Earl Warren and his allies — especially Justices William J. Brennan and William O. Douglas — had clearly stated that sections 241 and 242 of 18 *U.S.C.* were valid law and, if necessary, could be used in federal prosecutions.

Confessions and Names Named

On October 13, 1964, the FBI caught a break that would lead to the arrest and indictments of the Klansmen responsible for the planning and execution of Schwerner, Chaney, and Goodman. James Jordan, one of the Klansmen involved in the murders, confessed to FBI agents that he witnessed the killings and agreed to cooperate with the MIBURN investigation. After many conversations with FBI agent Proctor, he finally confessed and agreed to testify against his former friends and fellow Klansmen. Based on his information, less than two months later, eighteen Klansmen were arrested and charged with conspiracy to violate the civil rights of the three dead civil rights workers.

Evidently, Wallace Miller, a Lauderdale County Klansman, began cooperating with the FBI after the bodies were discovered. In his conversations with the agents he repeatedly mentioned James Jordan's name, indicating that Jordan was one of the killers and that he was very nervous and feared possible indictment and conviction for his part in the murders. Jordan moved in September to Gulfport, Mississippi, to take a job at a federal missile site and to get away from Neshoba County.

Proctor convinced Jordan to turn state's evidence. The FBI agent, working with information provided by informants, visited Jordan on the Mississippi coast. After five lengthy interviews with Proctor, Jordan finally confessed and named names of those involved in the killings. After his staged arrest by the FBI, Jordan and his family were relocated to Georgia. He was then brought back to Mississippi to work with the federal prosecutors in the presentation of information to the grand jurors and to testify for the prosecution. (At the federal trial in October 1967, he was the only prosecution witness to the shootings who took the stand to testify against the accused Klansmen.)

On November 5, 1964, Jordan signed a confession. It was, including a second interview by the FBI, a twenty-seven-page document that described in exhaustive detail the events that occurred from about 6:00 p.m. until after midnight on Sunday, June 21, 1964. Jordan's confession included all the names of the participants involved, from Deputy Sheriff Price's stop of the car, to Preacher Killen's careful planning of the seizure, the murder, and the burial of the civil rights workers.

An FBI report noted that Jordan, when looking at photographs shown to him by the FBI agents, "readily identified them as persons involved or having knowledge of the murders of the three civil rights workers in Neshoba County on June 21, 1964." The seventeen persons identified by Jordan included:

Bernard L. Akin, owner of Akin's Mobile Homes, who hosted Killen's meeting in Meridian the early evening of June 21, 1964 (his granddaughter Susan Akin was Miss America in 1986)

Earl B. Akin, worked with his relative Bernard Akin at the mobile homes

Jimmy Arledge, twenty-seven, Meridian truck driver

Horace Doyle Barnette, twenty-six, Meridian auto parts salesman

Travis Maryn Barnette, thirty-six, Meridian garage owner

Olen L. Burrage, thirty-five, trucking merchant, Neshoba County

James T. Harris, thirty, Meridian, investigator

Frank J. Herndon, manager, Meridian Longhorn Drive-In, KKK officer

Edgar Ray "Preacher" Killen, thirty-eight, Kleagle of Neshoba County Klavern, sawmill operator, Baptist preacher, obituary writer for the *Neshoba Democrat*

Billy Wayne Posey, thirty-six, gas station attendant, Philadelphia, Mississippi

Cecil Ray Price, twenty-six, deputy sheriff, Neshoba County

Lawrence Andrew Rainey, forty-one, sheriff, Neshoba County

Wayne Roberts, twenty-six, Meridian window salesman, ex-Marine (dishonorably discharged), bouncer in a local bar

Jerry Sharpe, twenty-one, manager of pulpwood supply company, Neshoba County

Jimmy Snowden, twenty-seven, Meridian truck driver

Jimmy Townsend, seventeen, Neshoba County, high school dropout, gas station attendant

Oliver Richard "Pops" Warner Jr., Meridian store owner

On November 19, 1964, after obtaining Jordan's information-laden confession, FBI agents Henry Rask and James A. Wooten visited

Horace Doyle Barnette, who had moved to Springhill, Louisiana, after the killings. The agents presented Barnette with the damning confession and were able to convince him to turn state's evidence as well.

His confession began with a telephone call from the Preacher: "The Klan had a job and wanted to know if . . . I could go. [I] did not know what the job was." Although not as exhaustively detailed as Jordan's, Barnette's statement corroborated the first confession in almost every detail. Jordan's confession, it turned out, did not detail Jordan's role in the shooting of J. E. Chaney; Barnette's did.

The FBI Arrests of Twenty-one Klansmen and the Dismissal of Charges

Armed with the two confessions, the FBI and the Department of Justice went into action. On December 4, 1964, twenty-one Klansmen (including Jordan, Barnette, and two additional persons, Otha Neal Burkes and Tommy Horne) were arrested by the FBI and charged with conspiring to violate the civil rights of Schwerner, Chaney, and Goodman (Section 241). That same day, the DOJ complaints were filed with the U.S. commissioner sitting in Meridian, Mississippi.

The hearing was held on December 10. Nineteen of the twenty-one men charged and arrested were there. Jordan and Barnette were arrested in Gulfport and Shreveport, Louisiana, respectively. The Meridian courtroom was packed, and more than 100 people stood outside the building. Deputy Sheriff Price was late in arriving. The reason: "It took me an hour to get [here] this morning. I had to shake so many hands," he said, a big grin on his face.

In the courtroom the accused were seen smiling, laughing, and generally seeming to enjoy their day in court. Sheriff Rainey was seated in the front row, smiling broadly, legs crossed, a wad of Red Man chewing tobacco in his mouth. His deputy, Cecil Price, was sitting next to him, also smiling. None of the accused Klansmen showed a shred of concern about the legal charges pressed against them by the federal government.

On this day, to the shock and chagrin of the DOJ lawyers, the U.S. commissioner in Meridian, Mississippi, Esther Carter, dismissed all charges at the preliminary hearing. She acted because the defense argued, and she accepted their argument, that the FBI's use of the written confession in the hearing — rather than presenting its author — was hearsay and hence inadmissible. The following account, from the FBI's MIBURN file, describes what happened:

> Commissioner Carter refused to allow FBI Agent Henry Rask to testify concerning a signed statement he received from Horace Doyle Barnette. Miss Carter ruled that Mr. Rask's testimony was hearsay and it would be necessary to produce the person who furnished the statement to testify as a witness. As a result of the Commissioner's ruling, Robert Owen, Departmental Attorney, U.S. DOJ, advised Miss Carter that the Government did not wish to present further evidence at the preliminary hearing. Miss Carter dismissed the complaint against the defendants.

Reactions to the commissioner's decision were as expected. The federal prosecutors were "shocked and dismayed at the unprecedented ruling made by Commissioner Carter," wrote Andrew Hopkins in his report to the Sovereignty Commission, dated December 11, 1964. He also noted that present in the courtroom were many "disappointed" COFO workers "wearing their freedom buttons and many of them were dressed in their usual dirty overalls, tennis shoes and boots, and needing a shave and haircut and bath badly. . . . [However], the majority of the white people in Meridian seemed to be well pleased that the charges against the defendants were dismissed."

The newspaper headlines in the Mississippi dailies trumpeted Carter's dismissal of all charges. The *Jackson Daily News* headline blared: "Dismiss Charges against 19 Men: Commissioner Acts Despite 'Confession.'" The *Jackson Clarion-Ledger* was equally pleased with the decision to dismiss the charges.

Federal Indictments of Eighteen Klansmen and the Dismissal of Charges

John Doar, Burke Marshall, Robert Owen, and other DOJ lawyers quickly got to work and, on January 1, 1965, presented data to a federal grand jury convened that day. Fifteen days later, the grand jurors sitting in Jackson issued a "true bill" charging eighteen Klansmen with violations of Title 18, *U.S.C.*, 241, 242, and 371 (conspiring to violate sections 241 and 242). (Jordan and Barnette were charged in other federal jurisdictions.)

On that day, January 15, 1965, warrants were issued for the arrest of the sixteen accused men then residing in the state. All were arrested the following day and arraigned before U.S. Commissioner Carter, who released them on $5,750 bond each. Barnette was arrested in Shreveport, Louisiana, arraigned, and then released on $5,000 bond. Jordan, also on January 16, voluntarily appeared at the Atlanta FBI office in response to the bench warrant, was arraigned, and then released on $5,000 bond.

The twelve defense attorneys, including five from Neshoba County, the entire legal community of Philadelphia, Mississippi, immediately filed a series of nine motions before U.S. District Court Judge Harold Cox. The first one was the crucial argument for the defendants, one that ultimately had to be resolved by the U.S. Supreme Court: "Motion to dismiss for lack of [federal] jurisdiction, as indictment does not allege a crime cognizable by the laws of the United States."

The judge who heard the motions and who was to hear the case at trial was William H. Cox, a former roommate at Ole Miss and still a close friend of powerful U.S. Senator Jim Eastland (D-Miss.). He was one half of the 1961 "deal" that saw Thurgood Marshall confirmed as a federal appeals court judge. Eastland, the chair of the Senate Judiciary Committee, told Bobby Kennedy that he could have his "nigger" if Cox could become a U.S. District Court judge. Five years later, the two federal employees would find themselves opposing each other in the *Price* case. Cox was an unregenerate racist who did all he could to delay desegregation actions by the federal government in his state. John Doar's experience with Cox in a March 1964 voter registration case was symptomatic of the judge's racism. Doar recalled the incident clearly:

I was in [Cox's] chambers on an application for a temporary injunction. I said to Judge Cox, "there's nothing un-American about blacks wanting to vote." Cox responded: [the black voter applicants] "were a bunch of chimpanzees." The offensive statement appeared the next day in a story in the *New York Times*. The resulting controversy nearly cost Cox his job. Senator Jacob Javits of New York and Congressman Peter Rodino of New Jersey led an impeachment effort. The attempt failed, but received substantial support.

Pretrial hearings were held from January 25 to 27, 1965, at the federal building in Meridian, Mississippi. Three motions presented by the defense were heard and argued before Judge Cox. These included a motion for severance, a motion to suppress search warrants, and a motion for the dismissal of the indictments against the Klansmen "on the basis they were prejudiced by undue publicity afforded in the preliminary hearing." All the witnesses who testified were defense witnesses. "No rebuttal testimony was presented by the Government," concluded the FBI report. Judge Cox "reserved decisions on these motions until a later unspecified date."

On February 24, 1965, Cox issued his order. He dismissed the Section 241 conspiracy charges and ruled that only the three law enforcement defendants could be tried under federal law for violating Section 242, a misdemeanor applicable only to those acting "under color of law" to deprive a person of due process. Cox's view of the conspiracy section (241) was very narrow and did not follow precedents already established by the U.S. Supreme Court in *Screws* and other cases that followed.

His first order was short, only four pages. Cox relied on the Court's *Cruikshank* decision of 1875, as well as the 1951 Supreme Court opinion *U.S. v. Williams* to dismiss the Section 241 charges against all defendants. As a lawyer, Cox knew that *Williams* was not the controlling case on the question of the breadth of Sections 241 and 242. However, given his clear sympathies in this litigation, his opinion freed the Klansmen from the more serious conspiracy charges. At the same time, Cox totally ignored the Court's more recent precedents, in *Screws* and in *Monroe*, that broadened the scope of the contested sections, 241 and 242, from the extremely narrow reading given to them by the *Cruikshank* Court. Erroneously, but purposefully, Cox said:

> This statute [Section 241] was designed and intended solely for the protection of federally created rights, not for any right merely guaranteed by the laws of the United States. This is not a statute which makes murder a federal crime under the facts and circumstances in this case. The right of every person not to be deprived

of his life or liberty without due process of law is a right that existed prior to the Federal Constitution. It is a right which is protected by state laws and is merely guaranteed by the Constitution of the United States. . . . The Fourteenth Amendment simply furnishes an additional guaranty against any encroachment by the States upon the fundamental rights which belong to every citizen as a member of society. . . . The defendants are not charged with the violation of any right which was conferred upon either [sic] of these victims by a federal law. . . . The indictment surely states a heinous crime against the State of Mississippi, but not a crime against the United States. This is a court of limited jurisdiction. The United States has no common law. . . . The indictment simply does not challenge either [sic] of these defendants with any offense against the laws of the United States. The motions to dismiss this indictment against the named defendants will, therefore, be sustained.

The following day, February 25, 1964, Cox ruled on the other motions presented by the defense. He indicated that the rest of the motions previously filed, with one exception, were "without merit and will be overruled." However, regarding Motion 3, in which the defendants "move to dismiss the indictment for failure to state an offense against, or a violation of any laws of the United States," specifically, (1) conspiring (Section 371) to violate Section 242, and (2) violating Section 242, he concluded that all eighteen Klansmen violated Section 371 in "that they all conspired to commit a crime against the United States under Section 371."

However, only the three law enforcement officers, Rainey, Price, and Philadelphia patrolman Willis, could be charged with violating Section 242. For the rest the charge was dismissed because they were at all times "private individuals," and as such were never acting "under color of law." Cox concluded: "The motion to dismiss the indictment will thus be sustained in part and overruled in part."

After Cox's two orders were handed down, the DOJ lawyers immediately filed an "expedited appeal" to the U.S. Supreme Court. In his brief for the federal government, newly appointed U.S. Solicitor General Thurgood Marshall wrote:

This case, as the members of the Court and, indeed, the entire country are aware, is one of extraordinary gravity and intrinsic importance. The public interest requires the prompt disposition of all the charges. Their prompt disposition, in accordance with the justice of the cause, depends upon the availability and recollection of key witnesses, either of which might be adversely affected by any substantial delay.

However, on March 15, 1965, the Supreme Court denied the request to hear the case as an accelerated appeal. Because it did not dismiss the appeal summarily, the case would be placed on the Court's docket in regular order. The justices would determine whether there was "probable jurisdiction" for them to review — by reviewing the case on its merits — Cox's interpretation of Sections 241 and 242 during its 1965–1966 term.

CHAPTER 5

U.S. v. Price in the U.S. Supreme Court

*This action [against the three civil rights workers] . . . was part of
a monstrous design. State officers [and other Klansmen] participated in every phase
of the alleged venture: the release from jail, the interception, assault, and murder.
It was a joint activity, from start to finish.*

JUSTICE ABE FORTAS, U.S. V. PRICE, MARCH 1966

In March 1965, the federal government presented its statement of
jurisdiction to the U.S. Supreme Court in No. 59, *U.S. v. Price, et al.*
(Section 241) and No. 60, *U.S. v. Price, et al.* (Section 242). In this
statement the government's brief argued that federal district court
judge Cox incorrectly answered an important question: "Whether
Section 241 of the Criminal Code encompasses Fourteenth Amendment Rights? . . . Since Section 241 is the only federal statute which
carries severe punishment for brutal physical violence in the invasion
of civil rights, its scope is a matter of grave concern," and both the
Congress and the executive branch "need a definitive interpretation
before determining the need for additional legislation."

The other question raised in the federal district court and by the
government in its appeal to the Supreme Court, in Number 60, was
"also important. . . . The district court — plainly and erroneously —
ruled that private persons without official status as state officers are
never amenable to Section 242 of the Criminal Code — albeit they
are intimately involved in the crimes of officials and are alleged themselves to be acting 'under color of law.'"

The statement asked the Court to consolidate the two cases, since,
in both, the same defendants were charged "out of the same course of
action." Further, the brief asked for expedited review because the case
"is one of extraordinary gravity and intrinsic importance." Then-solic-
itor general Archibald Cox (shortly thereafter replaced by Thurgood
Marshall) and Acting Assistant Attorney General for Civil Rights John
Doar were the two primary names on the government's statement of
jurisdiction.

Once again the justices tackled a constitutional and statutory conundrum they had been struggling with since the 1944 *Screws* litigation. Since then, the Court had had little success in defining the scope of Section 241. Did the Fourteenth Amendment itself, with its guarantees of "equal protection" and "due process" for all persons, fall within the parameters of Section 241's protective language?

The federal government argued that any infringement of these Fourteenth Amendment protections violated 241. Marshall's brief for the government asked the brethren to issue a "definitive definition" of the section that would end the protracted debate and uncertainty. Mississippi defense counsel in *Price* and the federal district court judge, however, disagreed with Marshall's position. Their counterargument was that 241's scope extended only to "legislatively created [national] rights" and did not extend to the Fourteenth Amendment protections.

The U.S. Supreme Court's Initial Response

On March 15, 1965, the Court denied the motion for an expedited review. The vote, according to Justice Douglas's conference notes, was 7:2. Only Justices Douglas and Harlan voted yes on the question of expediting the hearing of the case. However, the Court deferred other action "awaiting the timely filing of responses to the jurisdictional statement."

On April 26, after the brethren read the appellees' response, the Court announced that it would hear oral argument in the two cases: "Further consideration of the question of jurisdiction is postponed to the hearing of these cases on the merits. The motion to consolidate is granted and a total of two hours allotted for oral argument."

Both parties then submitted briefs on the merits, addressed to the questions raised by the government and by the Court: (1) Did the Court have jurisdiction to hear the case? (2) What was the scope of Section 241? (3) Under what circumstances, if any, could private persons be included in a Section 242 indictment charging them with acting "under color of law" to deprive persons of their Fourteenth Amendment rights?

The federal government's argument on the merits, with Thurgood

Marshall's signature on the brief, focused on one salient matter of great substance: "Whether the indictments — assuming the facts alleged can be proved — state offenses against the United States." In the brief and in oral argument, Solicitor General Marshall forcefully made the case that the indictments made proper use of Section 241. On both occasions, especially oral argument, he spoke and wrote directly about the scope of the conspiracy felony section, 241. Marshall's words were absolutely clear and went to the government's hoped-for answer to the questions raised in the case:

> The only question in this case is whether Section 241 encompasses 14th Amendment rights at all. That is not a constitutional question. At least since the *Screws* case, there can be no doubt whatever about the power of Congress to make it a federal crime for State officers to deprive citizens of their constitutional rights — even if the conduct also violates State law.

The appellees answered the question regarding Section 241 quite differently. Does Section 241 "encompass the due process clause of the Fourteenth Amendment, by an extension to an interference with the privileges and immunities of one citizen as against another citizen to be free of an assault and battery and/or murder inflicted by one citizen against another citizen?" The answer was not surprising: "Section 241 [only] extends to federally created rights."

> The right to be free of assault and battery as between one citizen and another or an assault and battery and murder by one citizen against another is not protected by the Fourteenth Amendment of the Constitution and is not reached by Section 241 of Title 18, *U.S.C.* and such is true as to a charge of conspiracy [Section 371] to commit false imprisonment, assault and murder. . . . The Fourteenth Amendment did not grant or create federal citizenship rights; it broadened the protection against encroachment by the State, but it did not add to or increase any right of one citizen against another, and the powers of the national government are limited to the enforcement of that guaranty.

Both briefs on the merits were filed with the Supreme Court in October 1965, the start of the 1965 term. By this time, the Warren Court was at its apex in its efforts to broaden fundamental rights and liberties of all persons in the United States. In the 1965 term, no fewer than four of the nine justices continually interpreted statutes and the phrases of the Constitution itself in a liberal — almost revolutionary — manner: Chief Justice Earl Warren and Associate Justices Douglas, William J. Brennan, and Arthur Goldberg (replaced, in 1965, by equally liberal Abe Fortas). Especially in civil rights litigation involving racial segregation, the quartet was usually joined by Associate Justices Byron White, Tom Clark, Hugo Black, and John M. Harlan II. Almost alone among the brethren, but certainly not isolated from the others on the issue, was Associate Justice Potter Stewart.

There were two personnel changes in the 1965 term. Associate Justice Arthur Goldberg resigned his seat to become the United States ambassador to the United Nations. On July 28, 1965, President Johnson filled Goldberg's seat with his longtime friend and confidant Abe Fortas. Over in the executive branch, Solicitor General Archibald Cox stepped down, and President Johnson appointed Thurgood Marshall, then serving as a federal appeals judge on the Second Circuit, U.S. Court of Appeals (CA2), to the important governmental position.

Marshall, as solicitor general, was "America's lawyer." It was, Marshall said many years later, the best job he ever had, including his more than two decades of service as an associate justice of the U.S. Supreme Court from 1967 to 1991.

On Monday, October 4, 1965, the opening day of the Court's 1965 term, Abe Fortas was introduced by Chief Justice Warren and took his official oath of office in open court. The following Monday, October 11, the chief justice took great pleasure in welcoming Thurgood Marshall, the incoming solicitor general, to the Court. Both men were highlighted in the *Price* litigation: Marshall argued the government's case before the Court; Fortas would be selected to write the opinion for the Court in the case.

Oral Argument and the U.S. Supreme Court's Initial Vote on the Merits

On November 9, oral argument took place in the Court's Marble Palace. Solicitor General Marshall, assisted by John Doar, presented the government's case to the justices. The appellees' arguments were presented to the brethren by Philadelphia, Mississippi, attorney Mike Watkins.

Thurgood Marshall was one of the three top civil rights advocates who argued cases in state and federal courts in the twentieth century. He loved this kind of lawyering, standing up and arguing a stated position vigorously — whether it was before a jury, a judge, a panel of judges, or the nine justices of the U.S. Supreme Court. While he was the NAACP's LDF chief litigator, from 1938 to 1961, he won thirty-nine of the forty-six cases the LDF brought before the Court.

On November 9 the oral argument was a walk in the park for Marshall. He was lobbed grapefruit-size softball questions by the justices, who clearly were very comfortable with the federal government's position. Marshall was in excellent form and the accomplished litigator batted quite well, hitting the softballs over the fence for home runs. He was so successful that Doar passed him a note: "I'm beginning to think more and more that you might do well to waive rebuttal." Marshall did just that, but not before he said, in his thunderous voice, the following (on his notes, Marshall clearly marked the passage: "s-l-o-w!"):

> The gravamen of both charges is the allegation of a conspiracy to willfully subject the victims to the deprivation of their rights, privilege and immunity secured and protected by the 14th Amendment to the Constitution of the United States. . . . [They were] not to be summarily punished without due process of law by persons acting under color of laws of the State of Mississippi.

On November 12, 1965, the Court discussed the case in its weekly conference session. Were the cases important enough for the Court to "note jurisdiction" and reach the merits of the issue? By an 8:1 vote in the conference, the Court noted jurisdiction. Then, after a discussion of the merits, by a vote of 9:0, the justices voted to overturn both of Cox's orders and to reinstate the indictments against the Klansmen.

The conversation in the conference session was less a debate than the voicing of an eight-person consensus. (The following paragraphs are based on the conference notes taken by Justices Brennan and Douglas.) Only Justice Stewart demurred — albeit briefly. He asked, rhetorically, "What is the 14th Amendment right that's involved here? Is murder such a violation? [I have] many other doubts [and] this leads me to wait until the whole [opinion is] written." In conference, the chief justice always begins the discussion of cases heard earlier that week in oral argument. Chief Justice Warren instantly said that he voted to reverse the Cox orders and to reinstate the indictments against the eighteen men — on both charges (241 and 242). "Section 242," he said, "applies to State officers *and those who associate with them.* [We] need both charged as aiders and abettors. *Screws* is relevant and [he] supports it" (my emphasis). The chief believed that "Congress intended things like this to come within the Act."

The senior associate justice, Hugo L. Black, also voted to reverse Cox. "The fifth paragraph of the 14th Amendment [giving Congress the power to 'enforce' the amendment by passing appropriate legislation] gives Congress the right to pass laws protecting racial groups." He "would, if necessary, overturn the [1883] *Civil Rights Cases* but probably [the Court] need not." In *Price*, he concluded, "there [is] no element of vagueness as in *Screws.*"

Justice Douglas, the author of the Court's *Screws* and *Monroe* majority opinions, voted to reverse the district court judge and did not say anything else. Justice Tom Clark, like Douglas, voted to reverse — as did Justice John M. Harlan Jr. For Harlan, the legislative history of Sections 241 and 241

such as there is, indicates Congress was talking in terms of the 14th Amendment rights, not the "natural" rights as such [discussed by Cox and was a significant portion of the appellees' arguments in the briefs and in front of the justices]. Once you say that 14th Amendment rights are covered, you have "state action" both in the conspiracy count and in the other count.

Justice Brennan voted to reverse, as did Justice Byron White and the junior Justice, Abe Fortas, who spoke and voted last. Only Justice Stewart was, as he told his colleagues that day, "not at rest." Three people were murdered, he said, and he asked, "What 14th Amendment right is involved?"

The consensus among the brethren was amazingly clear. With the exception of a hesitant, cautious Stewart — who stated he would await the draft opinion before he made a decision — the other eight were unanimous in their conclusion regarding the Cox orders. Equally important, they were unanimous in the justification for their decision to overturn the federal trial judge.

The chief assigned the new justice, Abe Fortas, to write the Court's opinion. It was unanimous; after reading the draft opinion circulated by Fortas, Justice Stewart quickly joined the others.

The Supreme Court Reaches Closure and Issues Its Order

In record time — only sixteen days after the oral arguments, on March 28, 1966— a unanimous opinion in the case of *U.S. v. Price, et. al.* was announced by its author, Abe Fortas. Justice Harlan, however, wrote a note to Fortas, asking that an important change be made in the draft opinion. Harlan asked that language in the draft be removed, for it suggested that 241 could reach private as well as governmental action. "Since this case does not face us with that question [the indictment under 241 identified three law enforcement officers working with fifteen private persons], I feel there should be no intimation on it one way or another." Fortas assented, and Harlan quickly "joined" the *Price* opinion.

For the Court, the "sole question presented in these appeals is whether the specified statutes make criminal the conduct for which the individuals were indicted. It was," wrote Fortas, echoing Marshall's point, "an issue of [statutory] construction, not of constitutional power." Congress has the right to enforce by appropriate criminal statutes "every right guaranteed by the Due Process Clause of the Fourteenth Amendment."

The junior justice, a close friend of Justice Douglas since they worked together in federal agencies in the early halcyon days of the Roosevelt New Deal, had cited Justice Douglas's observations in *U.S. v. Williams* — not Justice Frankfurter's much more narrow construction of 241 stated in that same case.

The eighteen Klansmen were not charged with assault or murder; the two indictments were "framed to fit the stated federal statutes, and the question before us is whether the attempt of the draftsman for the Grand Jury in Mississippi has been successful: whether the indictments charge offenses against the various defendants which may be prosecuted under [these statutes — 2 41 and 242]."

The Court first discussed the validity of the indictment based on

Section 242 ("under color of law") of the federal Criminal Code. It was written in 1866, Fortas explained, four years earlier than 241.

Judge Cox had dismissed three counts in the indictment — involving the fifteen "private" defendants — because the counts did not state that they were "officers in fact, or de facto in anything allegedly done by them 'under color of law.'" However, "we cannot agree" with Cox's dismissal of those counts against the fifteen Klansmen:

> Private persons, jointly engaged with state officials in the prohibited action, are acting "under color" of law for purposes of the statute. To act "under color" of law does not require that the accused be an officer of the State. It is enough that he is a willful participant in joint activity with the State or its agents. . . . This brutal joint adventure was made possible by state detention and calculated release of the prisoners by an officer of the State. State officers participated in every phase of the alleged venture: the release from jail, the interception, assault, and murder. It was a joint activity, from start to finish. . . . The contrary view in a Section 242 context was expressed by the dissenters in *Screws*, and was rejected then, later in *Williams* II, and finally — in a Section 1983 case — in *Monroe v Pape*.

The fault does not lie in the indictment, concluded the Court in this part of the *Price* decision, "but in the District Court's view that the statute requires that each offender be an official or that he act in an official capacity. . . . The trial court's determination of [the meaning of 'under color' of law] is in error." The Court reversed Cox's dismissal of the second, third, and fourth counts of the indictment in Number 60 "and remanded for trial."

Number 59 charged all eighteen Klansmen with a felony — a violation of Section 241: conspiring together

> to injure, oppress, threaten, and intimidate [Schwerner, Chaney, and Goodman] in the free exercise and enjoyment of the right and privilege secured to them by the Fourteenth Amendment to the Constitution of the United States not to be deprived of life or liberty without due process of law by persons acting under color of the laws of Mississippi.

Judge Cox dismissed the indictment against the eighteen Klansmen because he held that Section 241 does not include rights or privileges protected by the Fourteenth Amendment. The problem: Cox read Section 241 "with the gloss of [Frankfurter's opinion for four justices] *Williams* I." That was not how *Williams* should be read, concluded Fortas for the unanimous Court:

> We conclude that the District Court erred; that Section 241 must be read as it is written — to reach conspiracies "to injure . . . any citizen in the free exercise or enjoyment of any right or privilege secured to him by the Constitution or laws of the United States . . ."; that whatever the ultimate coverage of the section may be, it extends to conspiracies otherwise within the scope of this section, participated in by officials alone or in collaboration with private persons; and that the indictment in No. 59 properly charges such a conspiracy in violation of Section 241.

Again and again in *Price*, the Supreme Court — unanimously — "d[id] not agree" with Judge Cox. The language in Section 241, it said, "is plain and unlimited. . . . Its language embraces all of the rights and privileges secured to citizens by all of the Constitution and all of the laws of the United States." Unlike Judge Cox, "we are not at liberty to seek ingenious analytical instruments for excluding from [Section 241's] general language the Due Process Clause of the Fourteenth Amendment — particularly since the violent denial of legal process was one of the reasons motivating enactment of the section" in 1866 and again in 1870, two years after the Fourteenth Amendment was ratified.

The *Price* opinion of the Supreme Court clearly enunciated the breadth of the sections of 18 *U.S.C.* that had been rejected in federal district court. It was also an important decision that had a positive impact on the ability of the federal government to seek some kind of justice in these kinds of cases coming from the Deep South.

At the time, 1965, there was no federal criminal sanction to prosecute racially motivated acts of violence that were clearly intended to interfere with an individual's enjoyment of his or her federal rights. Until *Price*, there was still a bit of uncertainty about the ability of the federal prosecutors to use sections of post–Civil War Reconstruction statutes to indict Klansmen who committed acts of violence against civil rights workers.

The 1951 *Williams* precedents were problematic given their fractured nature. As Justice Fortas noted, "In view of the detailed opinions in *Williams* I, it would be supererogation to track the arguments in all of their intricacy." The *Price* opinion, a unanimous expression of the Supreme Court on the scope of Sections 241 and 242, gave the DOJ a weapon to use (by those who *wanted* to use these remedies) when local and state governments could not, or would not, bring to justice violent vigilante night-riding groups who assaulted others, bombed churches, and killed those they believed were the Antichrist.

The *Price* decision concluded with the Court's order: Cox's two judgments were "reversed and remanded." The indictments were once again operative. However, the game of evasion, avoidance, and delay on the part of the attorneys for the eighteen Klansmen — and Judge Cox himself — continued when action resumed in the federal U.S. District Court, Eastern Division, Southern District, Mississippi, in the fall of 1966.

Price provided the "definitive definition" of 241 to the legal and political communities by a unanimous Court. Fortas concluded that the section "reaches conspiracies to injure any citizen in the free exercise or enjoyment of *any* right or privilege secured to him by the Constitution or laws of the United States." Its language is "plain and unlimited." It "embraces *all* the rights and privileges secured to citizens by *all* of the Constitution and *all* of the laws of the United States." Period! End of debate, concluded the nine justices.

U.S. v. Guest: Another Section 241 Opinion, with a Twist and Partial Dissents

On the day that *Price* came down, another decision was announced in a case involving the murder of a black administrator by a group of Georgia Klansmen. Herbert Guest and five other members of the Athens, Georgia, Klavern were charged with criminal conspiracy, in violation of Section 241, in the July 11, 1964, murder of Lemuel Penn, a black U.S. Army reserve officer.

Lieutenant Colonel Penn was returning to his home in Washington, D.C., after a two-week military tour at a Georgia military base. The Klansmen were charged with a series of actions — over a period of more than a month, ending with the killing of Penn — which included damaging and destroying the property of black travelers, pursuing blacks in automobiles, threatening them with guns, providing state police with inaccurate information that caused the false arrest of blacks, and killing Penn during the course of their late night marauding on the state and interstate highways in and around Athens, Georgia.

However, unlike the fact situation in *Price*, the particulars in *Guest* showed that none of the six Klansmen was a law enforcement officer (there were three law enforcement officers involved in the conspiracy to kill the COFO trio). In September, 1964, after a Clarke County jury acquitted two of the Athens Klansmen in a state trial, the DOJ put together a Section 241 indictment against the Klansmen for conspiring to deprive Negro citizens in the vicinity of Athens, Georgia, of the free exercise and enjoyment of rights secured to them by the Constitution and laws of the United States, namely, the right to use state facilities without discrimination on the basis of race, the right freely to engage in interstate travel, and the right to equal enjoyment of privately owned places of public accommodation, now guaranteed by Title II of the Civil Rights Act of 1964.

The indictment specified various means by which the objects of the conspiracy would be achieved, including causing the arrest of Negroes by means of false reports of their criminal acts. The district court dismissed the indictment on the ground that it did not involve rights that are attributes of national citizenship, to which it deemed 241 solely applicable. The court also held the public-accommodation allegation legally inadequate for failure to allege discriminatory motivation, which the court thought essential to charge an interference with a right secured by Title II, and because the enforcement remedies in Title II were deemed exclusive. The United States appealed directly to the U.S. Supreme Court under the Criminal Appeals Act.

Guest addressed a somewhat similar and equally vexing question, one that had been discussed by the Supreme Court justices as early as the 1883 *Civil Rights Cases:* Did the Congress have the authority, under the "enforcement" section (5) of the Fourteenth Amendment, to punish private interference with a person's right to "equal protection" and "due process of law"? The 1883 majority said that the Fourteenth Amendment prohibits only "state action" that attempts to infringe the rights and privileges of persons protected by the amendment. The Court concluded that solely private action against an individual was actionable only in state proceedings.

Solicitor General Marshall once more argued the cause for the United States. With him on the brief was Assistant Attorney General Doar. The Court heard oral argument on November 9, 1965, and announced its decision on March 28, 1966, the same day *Price* was announced. The *Guest* decision was not unanimous, for three justices, the liberal trio of Chief Justice Warren and Justices Douglas and Brennan, felt that Stewart's opinion did not go far enough in its conclusion regarding Section 241.

Justice Potter Stewart, for the less than unanimous Court (there were four opinions handed down in the case), first held that "this Court has no jurisdiction under the Criminal Appeals Act to review the invalidation of that portion of the indictment concerning interference with the right to use public accommodations." Further, the Court said that the allegation by the DOJ in the indictment, of state involvement in the conspiracy charged under 241, was sufficient to charge a violation of rights protected by the Fourteenth Amendment. "Section 241 includes within its coverage Fourteenth Amendment rights whether arising under the Equal Protection Clause, as in this case, or under the Due Process Clause, as in *United States v. Price*." Section 241, wrote Stewart, is not unconstitutionally vague, since by virtue of its being a conspiracy statute it operates only against an offender acting with specific intent to infringe the right in question. Clearly, for Justice Stewart, the right to equal use of public facilities (state and interstate highways) was determined to be a definite right by many earlier decisions of the Supreme Court.

Further, Stewart noted that the state's involvement need be neither exclusive nor direct — but only "peripheral" — in order to trigger the rights in the Equal Protection Clause, and that the allegation concerning the arrest of Negroes by means of false reports was sufficiently broad to cover a charge of "active connivance" by state agents or other official discriminatory conduct constituting a denial of rights protected by the Equal Protection Clause.

Stewart's opinion for the majority avoided the main question raised by the federal government in *Guest*. It did so by finding in the facts of the case some "state action," albeit very marginal. Because of the division on the Court, *Guest* did not provide "definitive" guidance on the troublesome "state action" concept. The district court opinion dismissing the indictment "because Section 241 does not encompass any

Fourteenth Amendment rights . . . was in error," concluded Stewart. The judge's decision was reversed and remanded.

Justice Tom Clark, joined by Justices Black and Fortas, concurred. He did so to underline what he viewed was the well-crafted, prudential Stewart majority opinion. By acting carefully, the majority opinion "removes from the case any necessity for a 'determination' of the threshold level that state action must attain in order to create rights under the Equal Protection Clause." A study of the language in the indictment clearly shows that "the Court's construction is not a capricious one, and I therefore agree with that construction, as well as the conclusion that follows." Unlike Brennan's partial dissent, Clark believed that

> the Court's interpretation of the indictment clearly avoids the question whether Congress, by appropriate legislation, has the power to punish private conspiracies that interfere with Fourteenth Amendment rights, such as the right to utilize public facilities. . . . Some of my Brother Brennan's language . . . suggests that the Court indicates *sub silentio* that Congress does not have the power to outlaw such conspiracies. Although the Court specifically rejects any such connotation, it is, I believe, both appropriate and necessary under the circumstances here to say that there now can be no doubt that the specific language of Section 5 empowers the Congress to enact laws punishing all conspiracies — with or without state action — that interfere with Fourteenth Amendment rights."

Justice John M. Harlan II concurred in part and dissented in part.

> To the extent that [Part III of the majority opinion] is there held that 18 *U.S.C.* 241 reaches conspiracies, embracing only the action of private persons, to obstruct or otherwise interfere with the right of citizens freely to engage in interstate travel, I am constrained to dissent. On the other hand, I agree that 241 does embrace state interference with such interstate travel, and I therefore consider that this aspect of the indictment is sustainable on the reasoning of Part II of the Court's opinion.

Justice Brennan wrote an opinion, joined by Warren and Douglas, also concurring in part and dissenting in part. It took a dramatically different bent, one that — as Justice Clark pointed out in his concurring opinion—challenged the 1883 "state action" precedent announced in the *Civil Rights Cases.* Brennan did not agree with the majority opinion's view that

> a conspiracy to interfere with the exercise of the right to equal uti-
> lization of state facilities is not, within the meaning of Section 241,
> a conspiracy to interfere with the exercise of a "right secured by the
> Constitution" unless discriminatory conduct by state officers is
> involved in the alleged conspiracy. . . . I cannot agree with [Stewart's]
> construction of Section 241. I am of the opinion that a conspiracy to
> interfere with the right to equal utilization of state facilities . . . is a
> right "secured by the Constitution" *without regard to whether state
> officers participated in the alleged conspiracy.* . . . Section 241 reaches
> such a private conspiracy, not because the Fourteenth Amendment
> of its own force prohibits such a conspiracy, but because Section 241,
> as an exercise of congressional power under Section 5 of the Four-
> teenth Amendment, prohibits all conspiracies to interfere with a
> "right secured by the Constitution" and because the right to equal
> utilization of state facilities is a "right secured by the Constitution"
> within the meaning of that phrase as used in Section 241.

Had Justice Brennan received the support of just two other justices, the 1883 *Civil Rights Cases'* "state action" doctrine would have been shattered. Brennan's view, that Section 241, "as an exercise of congres-sional power under Section 5 of the Fourteenth Amendment, prohibits all conspiracies to interfere with a 'right secured by the Constitution,'" was in direct opposition to the nineteenth-century precedent.

His view, however, did not prevail. Because Justice Stewart noted some slight, "peripheral" state activity in the Klan's marauding and killing, the indictment was validated, and the Klansmen were brought to trial under the conspiracy charge. Justice Stewart also avoided any tampering with the 1883 "state action" precedent.

Because *Guest*, as well as the prosecution and appeal of those who were responsible for the murder of a civil rights worker in Alabama, Ms. Viola Liuzzo, in 1965 (*U.S. v. Wilkins, et al.*), did not answer the question of whether congressional powers extended to restraints on private action that deprived persons of their Fourteenth Amendment rights and privileges, the Johnson administration initiated legislative action to provide a definitive determination of the question via the legislative route.

The president created an ad hoc task force in the Civil Rights Division of the Department of Justice to draft the proposed legislation that would criminalize the actions of private individuals who conspired and acted to deprive other persons of their Fourteenth Amendment rights and privileges. Justice Clark's suggestion in his concurring opinion in *Guest* was taken to heart by the lawyers in that federal department.

Beginning with President Johnson's 1966 State of the Union message, the Johnson administration called repeatedly for the enactment of new legislation. In a Special Message to Congress dated April 28, 1966, Johnson proposed legislation to strengthen civil rights and *"to make [federal] authority against civil rights violence clear and sure"* (my emphasis).

The DOJ civil rights proposal Johnson later sent to Congress became the Civil Rights Act of 1968. It federally criminalized acts of racial violence related to the exercise of federal rights. Enacted into law as 18 *U.S.C.* Section 245, Federally Protected Activities, the 1968 Civil Rights Act was a major piece of legislation that protected a wide range of persons from denial of their constitutional and statutory rights by private persons as well as law enforcement officers.

The legislation began with a reflection of the nature of criminal justice systems in a federal system of government and of the importance of federal deference to the state's responsibility to develop and implement a fair criminal justice process:

(a)(1) Nothing in this section shall be construed as indicating an intent on the part of Congress to prevent any State, any possession or Commonwealth of the United States, or the District of Columbia, from exercising jurisdiction over any offense over which it would have jurisdiction in the absence of this section, nor shall anything in this section be construed as depriving State and local law enforcement authorities of responsibility for prosecuting acts that may be violations of this section and that are violations of State and local law. No prosecution of any offense described in this section shall be undertaken by the United States except upon the certification in writing of the Attorney General, the Deputy Attorney General, the Associate Attorney General, or any Assistant Attorney General specially designated by the Attorney General that in his judgment a prosecution by the United States is in the public interest and necessary to secure substantial justice, which function of certification may not be delegated.

The statute gave extremely broad powers to the DOJ to take action against any person "whether or not acting under color of law, [who] by force or threat of force willfully injures, intimidates or interferes with, or attempts to injure, intimidate or interfere with" the following:

(1) any person because he is or has been, or in order to intimidate such person or any other person or any class of persons from

(A) voting or qualifying to vote, qualifying or campaigning as a candidate for elective office, or qualifying or acting as a poll watcher, or any legally authorized election official, in any primary, special, or general election

(B) participating in or enjoying any benefit, service, privilege, program, facility, or activity provided or administered by the United States;

(C) applying for or enjoying employment, or any perquisite thereof, by any agency of the United States;

(D) serving, or attending upon any court in connection with possible service, as a grand or petit juror in any court of the United States;

(E) participating in or enjoying the benefits of any program or activity receiving Federal financial assistance; or

(2) any person because of his race, color, religion or national origin and because he is or has been

(A) enrolling in or attending any public school or public college;

(B) participating in or enjoying any benefit, service, privilege, program, facility or activity provided or administered by any State or subdivision thereof;

(C) applying for or enjoying employment, or any perquisite thereof, by any private employer or any agency of any State or subdivision thereof, or joining or using the services or advantages of any labor organization, hiring hall, or employment agency;

(D) serving, or attending upon any court of any State in connection with possible service, as a grand or petit juror;

(E) traveling in or using any facility of interstate commerce, or using any vehicle, terminal, or facility of any common carrier by motor, rail, water, or air;

(F) enjoying the goods, services, facilities, privileges, advantages, or accommodations of any inn, hotel, motel, or other establishment which provides lodging to transient guests, or of any restaurant, cafeteria, lunchroom, lunch counter, soda fountain, or other facility which serves the public and which is principally engaged in selling food or beverages for consumption on the premises, or of any gasoline station, or of any motion picture house, theater, concert hall, sports arena, stadium, or any other place of exhibition or entertainment which serves the public, or of any other establishment which serves the public and (i) which is located within the premises of any of the aforesaid establishments or within the premises of which is physically located any of the aforesaid establishments, and (ii) which holds itself out as serving patrons of such establishments; or

(3) during or incident to a riot or civil disorder, any person engaged in a business in commerce or affecting commerce including, but not limited to, any person engaged in a business which sells or offers for sale to interstate travelers a substantial portion of the articles, commodities, or services which it sells or where a substantial portion of the articles or commodities which it sells or offers for sale have moved in commerce; or

(4) any person because he is or has been, or in order to intimidate such person or any other person or any class of persons from

(A) participating, without discrimination on account of race, color, religion or national origin, in any of the benefits or activities described in subparagraphs (1)(A) through (1)(E) or subparagraphs (2)(A) through (2)(F); or

(B) affording another person or class of persons opportunity or protection to so participate, or such citizen or any other citizen from lawfully aiding; or encouraging other persons to participate, without discrimination on account of race, color, religion or national origin, in any of the benefits or activities described in subparagraphs (1)(A) through (1)(E) or subparagraphs (2)(A) through (2)(F), or participating lawfully in speech or peaceful assembly opposing any denial of the opportunity to so participate.

Under 18 *U.S.C.* 245, the penalty for a person found guilty of acting to deny another person any of the preceding protected rights was much more severe than the sanctions and penalties in Sections 241 and 242. The nominal penalty was a fine or imprisonment for one year. However, "if bodily injury results from the acts committed in violation of this section or if such acts include the use, attempted use, or threatened use of a dangerous weapon, explosives, or fire, shall be fined under this title, or imprisoned not more than ten years, or both."

If, as was the case in *Price, Guest,* and *Wilkins,* "death results from the acts committed in violation of this section or if such acts include kidnapping or an attempt to kidnap, aggravated sexual abuse or an attempt to commit aggravated sexual abuse, or an attempt to kill," the guilty person "shall be fined under this title or imprisoned for any term of years or for life, or both, or may be sentenced to death."

Price Returns to the U.S. Federal District Court

The *Price* case went back to the U.S. District Court, Eastern Division, Southern District. Once again, however, the constitutionality of the indictments was challenged by defense counsel. Its argument: the composition of the grand jury that returned the indictments, all-white males, violated the Constitution because the grand jury panel did not have any women or blacks on it! Ironically, once again, in September 1966, Judge Cox dismissed the indictments.

The DOJ lawyers did not appeal the ruling. Instead, they obtained another set of indictments on February 26, 1967, charging eighteen Klansmen with a Section 241 conspiracy. In this final indictment, the DOJ lawyers did not attempt to secure Section 242 ("under color of law") indictments. Selling the conspiracy case was a fairly clear matter. The DOJ did not want to jeopardize its case with the somewhat murky "under color of law" section. Besides, it was only a misdemeanor offense. Judge Cox could not do anything with the new indictments, given the U.S. Supreme Court's *Price* ruling and the fairly impaneled grand jury panel that voted out the new indictments against the Klansmen.

At last the trial date was set: May 26, 1967. However, Judge Cox acquiesced when the defense asked for additional time to prepare its defense, and the trial was postponed until October 1967.

CHAPTER 6

The Trial in Federal District Court

They killed one nigger, one Jew, and a white man [sic].
I gave them all what I thought they deserved.
JUDGE HAROLD COX, DECEMBER 1967

When the trial finally began, in early October 1967, in the Eastern Division, Southern District, Mississippi, U.S. District Court, three years, two months, and five days had passed since the bodies of Schwerner, Chaney, and Goodman were found on August 4, 1964. By the time the trial began, there had been three fund-raising dinners for the eighteen Klansmen charged with conspiring to murder the three civil rights workers. The biggest bash was the Jackson, Mississippi, event, where several hundred Mississippians paid $30 a plate for the honor of supporting the defense in the upcoming trial. (Interestingly, more than $5,000 of the funds raised for the defendants somehow "disappeared," much to their chagrin.)

Judge Cox, however, was still the trial judge, and the jury trial was to take place in his courtroom. The judge was then in his early sixties, with gray hair and deep blue eyes. He was a commanding segregationist presence in his court. Len Holt, one of the COFO lawyers involved in the planning and implementation of the Mississippi Freedom Summer project, recalled the large mural above the bench in Judge Cox's courtroom:

> Gazing from left to right, the visitor would have seen the slaves picking cotton and getting their bags weighed by a white overseer. Next he would have seen . . . a tall white man with a broad-brimmed hat with his right arm in front of a white woman holding a baby while a girl with blond hair, appearing to be about 10 years of age, stands nearby. With his left hand, the tall white planter helps an aged white woman — in black with shoulders draped — maintain her delicate stance. And then there is an equally tall white minister looking learned and holding the "holy book." To the minister's left is a collection of young white men reading blueprints and con-

structing a building which contrasts sharply with the shabbiness of the slave shack at the opposite side of the painting. Underneath the mural would sit Judge Cox.

On Monday, October 9, 1967, the trial of the Klansmen began. Across the square from the federal courthouse, in front of a barber shop facing the court building, Raymond Roberts, the brother of Wayne Roberts, the Klansman who killed all three young men, hung up a huge Confederate flag to the sounds of cheering from onlookers.

The Jury Is Impaneled and the Trial Begins

Prior to the beginning of the trial, John Doar and the federal government won a major victory from Judge Cox. Doar requested and, surprisingly, Judge Cox granted the prosecution motion that the juror pool be drawn from the entire Southern Mississippi District rather than from just the six counties surrounding Neshoba County, including Lauderdale County, as the twelve defense counsel had requested. The federal prosecutor was relieved and said afterward that the government "would never have had a chance with a jury from those counties around Neshoba."

The juror pool consisted of more than 200 persons, including 17 blacks. Defense peremptory challenges led to the exclusion of all of them. A white juror who admitted being a member of the KKK "a couple of years ago" was challenged for cause by the federal prosecutors. Judge Cox, however, denied the challenge. In a *voire dire* proceedings (where jurors are selected for the trial), counsel for both sides have "peremptory" challenges and challenges "for cause" they employ to remove jurors they believe may not act fairly. A peremptory challenge to a juror allows the lawyer to excuse the person without any assignment of reason or cause. A challenge for cause, however, is when the lawyer objects to a potential juror by pointing out the grounds upon which the juror is disqualified because he or she cannot act fairly. In the latter motion, the trial judge makes the determination.

By the end of the first day, an all-white jury of seven women and five men — ranging in age from thirty-four to sixty-seven years — was chosen. Most came from a working-class background: electricians, laborers, a cook, a pipe fitter, and a textile worker were represented on the jury. The jury foreman was Langdon Smith Anderson, fifty-two years old, from Lumberton, Mississippi. He was an oil exploration operator and a member of the State Agricultural and Industrial Board. The other members of the jury were as follows:

Willie V. Arnesen, fifty-eight, Meridian, secretary
Adelaide H. Comer, forty-three, Ocean Springs, school cafeteria cook
Mrs. Nell B. Dedeaux, forty-two, Poplarville, housewife
Mrs. S. M. Green, sixty-seven, Hattiesburg, housewife
Mrs. James C. Heflin, forty-eight, Lake, production worker
Jessie P. Hollingsworth, forty-eight, Moss Point, electrician
Mrs. Lessie Lowery, fifty-two, Hiwannee, grocery store owner
Edsell Z. Parks, thirty-four, Brandon, clerk
Harmon W. Rasberry, fifty-two, Stonewall, textile worker
Mrs. Gussie B. Staton, sixty-four, Union, housewife
Howard O. Winborn, fifty-six, Petal, pipe fitter

William Bradford Huie, a southerner by birth and the author of *Three Lives for Mississippi*, was covering the trial for the *New York Herald Tribune*. He thought that a guilty verdict was nearly impossible given the backgrounds of the jurors chosen to hear the evidence and then to determine guilt or innocence. Of the jurors, he wrote: "These are little people. Some of them are quite poor. Some of them live on the edges of small communities, far back in the piney woods. How can they afford to take the risks?"

The eighteen Klansmen were present in court with their dozen defense counsel. One of them, an ailing Frank Herndon, was clad in his pajamas and a bathrobe, and sitting next to him was "a lady nurse." Except for the Neshoba County attorney, the entire cohort of Neshoba County lawyers (five) defended the men from their county. A Jackson, Mississippi, attorney defended Sheriff Rainey. Five Meridian lawyers represented the Lauderdale County Klansmen. Imperial Wizard Bowers had his own counsel, Travis Buckley. The following men were indicted by the federal grand jury:

Bernard Akin	Edgar Ray "Preacher" Killen
Jimmy Arledge	Billy Wayne Posey

E. G. "Hop" Barnett	Cecil Ray Price
Horace Doyle Barnette	Lawrence Rainey
Travis Barnette	Wayne Roberts
Sam Bowers	Jerry Sharpe
Olen Burrage	Jimmy Snowden
James "Pete" Harris	Herman Tucker
Frank Herndon	Richard Willis

Almost three and one-half years after the three young men were brutally murdered, a criminal trial — although not a capital case — was about to commence in a Mississippi courtroom. Clearly, this event was a rarity in the Deep South, for so many earlier killers had either escaped a trial altogether or were either acquitted or freed because of a hung jury. Huie's reflection on the outcome of the trial was the common one. No one had ever been convicted of murdering a black man or white civil rights workers in the state of Mississippi. And there was no reason to believe that that record of impunity from justice would be broken in 1967.

The Trial of Cecil Price and Others for Conspiracy

The trial itself, from jury selection and opening arguments to the concluding arguments, lasted nine days. A total of 160 witnesses appeared before the jury during the five days of testimony. The great majority of them, 114, were defense witnesses (only one defendant took the stand in his own defense) who testified to the "good moral character" of the defendants or provided alibis for some of them, including the Preacher.

The unannounced but very clear strategy of the defense counsel was to lean heavily on the trial judge himself for favorable rulings. The great fear of the prosecutors was that Cox would continue to express his racist beliefs in rulings from the bench. The fact that Cox ruled in favor of the prosecution's request for the larger juror pool sent a clear message to the defendants and the lawyers. It was a very unsettling ruling for the dozen defense counsel; at the same time, it was an extremely pleasing one for Doar and the two other federal lawyers. Seemingly, Cox's recent near impeachment in the U.S. House of Representatives had left an impression on the sixty-plus-year-old Mississippi jurist.

John Doar presented a short opening statement to the court. After telling the jurors that the defendants conspired to murder the three young men "because they didn't like what these boys stood for," he explained why the federal government, rather than Mississippi, filed charges against the eighteen:

> I hope very much that you will understand the reason I have come here. It's not because of any skilled experience that I am here, but only because I hold the office as head of the division with the DOJ, and it is my responsibility to try and enforce the law in which these defendants have been charged. . . . I am here because your national government is concerned about your local law enforcement and in a civilization local law must work if we deserve our liberty and freedom. [However], when local law enforcement officials become involved as participants in violent crime and use their position, power, and authority to accomplish this, there is very little to be hoped for, except with assistance from the federal government.

Doar told the court that the federal government was "not invading Philadelphia or Neshoba County, Mississippi." The eighteen Klansmen were being tried for a crime "under federal law in a Mississippi city, before a Mississippi judge, in a Mississippi courtroom before twelve men and women from the State of Mississippi. The sole responsibility of the determination of guilt or innocence of these men remains in the hands where it should remain, the hands of twelve citizens from the State of Mississippi." Most of the defense counsel followed with an array of short opening statements about the innocence of their clients. One attorney opened by telling the court that John Doar was the same federal lawyer who "forced the Negro James Meredith into the University of Mississippi."

The prosecution presented its nineteen witnesses in two sets. The larger group provided background information, such as details about Mickey and Rita Schwerner's arrival in Meridian, Mississippi, in late January 1964; about Mickey's creative work on behalf of blacks in the county; about his visits to local black churches in Lauderdale and Neshoba Counties, seeking places to conduct voter registration programs and set up Freedom Schools for the Freedom Summer project.

Ernest Kirkland, a black resident of Neshoba County, spoke about his conversation with Schwerner and the others on Sunday afternoon, June 21, at the site of the burned-out Mount Zion Methodist Church. He described what the young men were wearing and his recollection of seeing them off as they left on their return trip to Meridian.

A Mississippi state policeman, E. R. Poe, spoke about Deputy Sheriff Price's stop of the trio on Highway 19 in the late afternoon of June 21, just inside the Philadelphia town limit. Minnie Herring, the wife of the Neshoba County jailer, in whose jail Schwerner, Chaney, and Goodman were kept from about 6:00 P.M. until their fateful release at 10:30 P.M. that night, related to the court that Price came into the jail at about 10:30 to tell her that he was releasing the three men.

These witnesses also included the Reverend Charles Johnson, who spoke about Schwerner's work as CORE leader in Meridian, Mississippi. He testified that Schwerner worked on "voter registration, organized boycott of stores to get better jobs [for blacks], upgrading of employment, better education, [and] also police treatment of negroes." On cross-examination, Johnson was asked by Laural Weir, the lead defense counsel, a number of somewhat outrageous questions: Was Schwerner an atheist? Did Schwerner advocate the burning of draft cards? Getting out of Vietnam? Did Schwerner ever travel to Cuba?

A second major blow to the defense again came from their erstwhile friend, Judge Harold Cox. On cross-examination of Johnson, Laurel Weir asked questions that tried to show that Schwerner was an indecent, hateful, atheistic anarchist. He went too far, however, when he asked Johnson the following:

WEIR: Now, let me ask you if you and Mr. Schwerner didn't advocate and try to get young male Negroes to sign statements agreeing to rape a white woman a week during the hot summer of '64?

COX: [Allowed the question over objection from the prosecuting attorneys. Cox told them, "I am going to let him answer the question."]

JOHNSON: No, never. . . .

COX: Counsel, you ought to have a good basis for a question like that. It would be a highly improper question [unless counsel] had a good basis for it. [What is] some basis for that question in this record[?]

WEIR: A note was passed to me by someone else.

COX: Well, who is the author of that question? . . . Which of you passed that question up?

HERMAN ALFORD (another defense counsel): Brother Killen wrote the question, one of the defendants.

COX: All right, I'm not going to allow a farce to be made of this trial and everybody might as well get that through their heads, including every one of these defendants, right now! I don't understand such a question as that, and I don't appreciate it, and I'm going to say so before I get through with the trial of this case. . . . I'm surprised at a question like that coming from a preacher, too. I'm talking about Killen, or whatever his name is.

After the trial ended, Doar said that the rape question "was the second big turning point. If there had been any feeling in the courtroom that the defendants were invulnerable to conviction in Mississippi, the incident dispelled it completely. Cox made it clear he was taking the trial seriously. That made the jurors stop and think: 'If Judge Cox is taking this stand, we'd better meet our responsibility as well.'" (Another courtroom observer that day was a local, a member of the Neshoba County Board of Supervisors. He said, simply, "The judge got mad that first day, and stayed mad the rest of the time.")

The second group of witnesses for the prosecution were two FBI informants, Mississippians who had joined the KKK but were subsequently repelled by the plans of the Lauderdale and Neshoba Klaverns to commit arson and assault and, after Bowers's order of April 1964, to eliminate Goatee Schwerner. The two men, Carlton Wallace Miller and Delmar Dennis, quit the Klan. Subsequently, they were persuaded by FBI agents to continue their involvement in the Klan — but as paid informants of the FBI. Miller and Dennis became featured witnesses for the federal government. Each was able to talk about his firsthand knowledge of the events of June 21, 1964. Doar told the court:

> Faced with this wall of silence [in Lauderdale and Neshoba Counties], the FBI encouraged Miller to step forward and furnish what he had heard from his friends within the Klan, and to appeal to Delmar Dennis to penetrate the hierarchy of the plan and to reveal their secrets, believing that this would lead to fixing the responsibility on all of those who planned this crime. All of you [jurors] probably have

an initial resentment against paid informers, but before you finally decide, examine these men, Miller and Dennis. They are native sons of Mississippi, they are men of courage, because who among us would doubt their lives are constantly in danger?

Miller, a forty-three-year-old, twenty-year veteran sergeant on the Meridian, Mississippi, police force, told the jurors about the organization of the Lauderdale Klavern, what he had heard while in the Klan, and about his conversations with its leaders, including Kleagle Edgar Ray "Preacher" Killen. He told reporters at the time of the trial, "It's hard to have to sit there and point your fingers at relatives and people you've known for a long time. It's hard." He also spoke of the various "pressures" applied by the Klan on black supporters of civil rights activities:

> DOAR: What were the various types of pressures?
> MILLER: To begin with, we were to call them up or go to see them and threaten them on their jobs and things of that nature.
> COX: Go to see whom?
> MILLER: Their bosses.
> DOAR: Was there any other kind of pressure discussed?
> MILLER: Whipping and beatings. . . . After the pressure was applied and they didn't respond then we were to resort to physical pressure if we wanted to whip someone the [Klavern] would vote on it and then the Exalted Cyclops would either reject it or OK the beating.
> DOAR: Now, was there any other action?
> MILLER: There was elimination.
> DOAR: What does elimination mean?
> MILLER: Murder.
> DOAR: Now, how did that have to be approved?
> MILLER: That had to be approved by the Imperial Wizard [Bowers]. If [he] wanted them disposed of he would turn that over to the Kleagle [Preacher Killen]. . . . Prior to the June 16th meeting [after the Klan visited the Mount Zion Methodist Church], they [the Klan] wanted to whip Schwerner, but they reported that they hadn't been able to see him. Mr. Killen told us to leave him alone that another unit was going to take care of him, that his elimination had been approved [by Bowers]. . . .

DOAR: Did Mr. Herndon tell you anything further about the missing civil rights workers?

MILLER: [He] told me that someone goofed up that they were supposed to carry that car [CORE's station wagon used by Schwerner] to Birmingham, Alabama.

DOAR: Did you have any conversation with Mr. Killen after June 21 about the three missing civil rights workers?

MILLER: He told me that they had been shot, that they were dead, and that they were buried in a dam about 15 feet deep, and he told me that Deputy Price told the FBI the truth about what time he turned them out [of the jail].

Delmar Dennis, a twenty-four-year-old Baptist and Methodist minister (he began preaching when he was fourteen years old), was the Meridian Klavern's Kludd, or chaplain. Shortly after joining the Klan, Dennis was appointed the Province Titan, the administrative officer who represented the Imperial Wizard, Bowers. Dennis quit the Klan after hearing about the plan to murder Schwerner, and at the trial he incriminated Sam Bowers. Dennis testified that, after the killings, Bowers told him that "it was the first time that Christians had planned and carried out the execution of a Jew." He also said that Bowers was absolutely unconcerned about the upcoming trial. "He said," testified Dennis, "Judge Cox would probably make them take [the three bodies] and put them back under the dam — that it was an illegal search [conducted by the FBI]." At the end of his testimony, Dennis pointed to one of the twelve defense counsel, Clayton Lewis, then the mayor of Philadelphia, and told the court that the Neshoba County Klavern held meetings on a pasture owned by Lewis, who was also a member of the Klan.

Laurel Weir cross-examined Dennis and it was, naturally, a bitter, angry defense counsel who asked questions. At one point, Weir tried to paint the young minister as a Judas: "Instead of 30 pieces of silver, you got $15,000!" Cox immediately reprimanded the defense counsel, who then sat down.

The last witness for the prosecution was Jim Jordan. He was the only witness who was at the scene of the murders, was able to provide the jurors with eyewitness testimony about the events surrounding the killing and burial of Schwerner, Chaney, and Goodman from about

6:00 P.M., June 21, to 1:00 A.M., June 22, 1964. On the day he was to testify, Jordan was flown in from Georgia, where he had been relocated, and escorted into the federal courthouse by five FBI agents, carrying their guns to protect him from possible assassination by the Klan.

Jordan told the jury that initially the Lauderdale Klan wanted Schwerner locked up and whipped because he "needed his rear end tore up." He also testified that there was a mistake made regarding the disposition of the station wagon driven by Chaney on that fateful day in late June:

> DOAR: What about the disposal of the station wagon?
> JORDAN: He said the station wagon, don't worry about it, it would be taken to Alabama and burned.
> DOAR: Did he indicate to you the name of the [driver]?
> JORDAN: He said, "Herman will take it to Alabama," is all I know.

It was the defense's turn to present evidence to the jury showing that the eighteen Klansmen did not conspire to murder the three civil rights workers. They paraded 113 witnesses before the jurors, "the salt of the earth kind of people," Laurel Weir called them. All testified about the virtues of the defendants or provided alibis for some of them. "Sam [Bowers]," said one, "is in church every time the doors are open. I believe Sam has had an experience with the Lord." Preacher Killen's friends said that Killen was at a funeral home paying his respects to a departed uncle at the time of the killings, and so on. Altogether the witnesses provided alibis for thirteen of the eighteen defendants.

Weir compared his people with those who testified for the prosecution. The federal government's infiltration strategy (nearly 20 percent of the Mississippi Klan's membership were FBI informants), he stated, was similar to the Soviet Union's system of "neighbors informing on neighbors."

Mike Watkins, another defense attorney, attempted to persuade the jurors that "Mississippians rightly resent some hairy beatniks from another state visiting our state with hate and defying our people. [They are not civil rights workers] but low-class riff-raff, misfits in our own land." Further, the federal government's case was an effort to use the government's mighty "central power" to intimidate innocent, peaceful Mississippians.

Closing Arguments of the Federal Government and the Defendants

On Wednesday, October 18, 1967, the ninth day of the trial, concluding arguments were presented by opposing counsel. John Doar's argument was a very careful step-by-step examination of the events that took place on June 21 and 22, 1964. It was a painful process, interrupted occasionally by objections by the defense counsel. Doar carefully explained the structure and functions of the White Knights of the Mississippi KKK:

> This was no Boy Scout Group, it was here to do business. There would be certain things the Klan would need to do, its members learned. Cross-burnings, meetings, and eliminations, provided that discipline was maintained and that of this type of action was approved by the local State organization. [Doar then quoted a statement issued by Sam Bowers]: "As Christian militants, we are disposed to use our physical force against our enemies." It says, "our enemies should be humiliated and driven out of the community by propaganda well enough, but if they continue to resist, they must be physically destroyed. The Klan must never give the enemy an even break, it is a life and death struggle and we must at all times be ready and strive and break and destroy our enemies."

After talking about the Klan, Doar reassessed the conspiracy that led to the murders of the three young civil rights workers. He said that members of a conspiracy usually play "different parts. There are the master planners, there are the organizers, there are the look-out men, there are the killers, there are the clean-up and disposal people, and there are the protectors." Doar once again described how each of the eighteen defendants fit into this scenario—from Bowers, the master planner, to Killen, the organizer, to Jordan and "Hop" Barnette as the lookouts, to Roberts, the killer, and to Herndon, the disposal Klansman. Doar then concluded his summation:

> Members of the jury, this is an important case. It is important to the government. It's important to the defendants, but most important, it's important to the State of Mississippi. What I say, what the

other lawyers say here today, what the Court says about the law will soon be forgotten, but what you twelve people do here today will be long remembered. . . . The defendants will beg of you for indulgence. In effect they will say as [Shakespeare's] Gloucester said of old as he stood over the body of his slain king, he begged the queen "say I slew him not." The queen replied, "then say they were not slain, but they are dead." If you find that these men or that each of them is not guilty of this conspiracy, it would be as true to say that there was no night time release from jail by Cecil Price, that there were no White Knights, there are no young men dead, there was no murder. If you find that these men are not guilty, you will declare the law of Neshoba County to be the law of the State of Mississippi.

It was now the defense's turn. Eleven of the twelve lawyers for the Klansmen had something to say to the jurors. W. D. Moore complained to the jury that the federal government "brought in its crack leader-organizer John Doar . . . and then they opened up the coffers of the United States for money [to pay the informers]." This prosecution, he argued, was because the president, the vice president, and Senator Robert Kennedy "instigated it." Herman Alford's closing was simple: the defendants, he uttered sincerely, "are as innocent and pure as the driven snow."

Mike Watkins was the last defense attorney to speak to the jurors. He pointed out that "every single one of the defendants proved their whereabouts. Relatives and friends [testified] to their whereabouts."

Mrs. Carrie Benton, testified for Frank Herndon. Would you stand up Frank? [He] was portrayed by the government in this case as a man who planned an audacious murder. You may sit down Frank. What did Mrs. Benton say, where did she say he was. Members of the jury, I never ask ladies what their age is, but Mrs. Benton came here and took the stand and in my judgment she is fifty-seven or sixty years of age. [Did] that lady come up and hold her hand [up] and swear a lie? Can you tell yourself that Frank Herndon was on that night planning to murder? What type of person was he according to Mrs. Benton? He was a man going back and forth to his place of business in attendance with Mrs. Benton, a two month old child, not a two year old child, members of the jury, but a two month old child. Bring the child milk and bringing Mrs. Benton supper. Did you hear that type of testimony from paid informers? No, I tell you that a man that is in attendance with a two month old child just doesn't have those characteristics of going out and planning murders. . . . Every single one of these defendants produced the same type of witnesses. You are called upon to disregard every single one of them and follow the so-called theory of a conspiracy case which is nothing more then that this is what he said, a midnight murder, that he wants you to overshadow and think it is.

These many defense witnesses, he said, were friends and relatives of the defendants. "At least they're not paid informers. . . . If life in Mississippi is miserable for the agitators who come here, it's because they made it that way." He concluded his summation by again speculating that even the deaths of the three civil rights workers were the responsibility of the COFO.

We do not know who the killers are, that's 1964. Members of the jury, it may well be that these young men were sacrificed by their own kind for publicity or other reasons. . . . Members of the jury, I ask you to please do one thing, and I believe the Court would ask you to do the same things, and that is that you vote your own conviction in this case. . . . Hold on to your own convictions. . . . There is reasonable doubt, you must keep it that way and beware, and justice may be done. It's so much better and I think the law provides that a thousand guilty ones go free than one innocent defendant here be convicted. I place the welfare of my clients in your hands. Thank you.

The last person to address the jurors was a Mississippian, Robert Hauberg, a U.S. attorney. He spoke briefly about the fundamental principle he lived by, one that he learned growing up in Mississippi: "A complete respect for law and authority."

At about 4:30 P.M. on October 18, 1967, the case went to the jury. The consensus view of reporters and citizens in the courtroom was that the jury would acquit all eighteen men. For Huie, the *New York Herald-Tribune* reporter (born in the South), a guilty vote was impossible.

The Verdict and the Sentences

The members of the jury deliberated for almost five hours on October 18 and then were bedded down in the Lamar Hotel in Meridian. The following day, they continued talking until about 3:00 P.M., when they reported to Judge Cox that they had reached an impasse. He then read them the "Allen charge" in an effort to end the deadlock. This is an instruction approved by the U.S. Supreme Court in *Allen v. U.S.*, that the jurors should examine the questions given to them by the judge "with candor and with a proper regard and reference to the opinions of each other." Cox reminded the jurors of the expenses involved in conducting a second trial if the jury was unable to reach a decision, and that it was fine if jurors changed their opinions when the discussion continued.

The jurors went back to work. While they were deliberating, an officer of the court overheard Wayne Roberts, standing in the hallway, tell Cecil Price that "Judge Cox just gave that jury a 'dynamite charge.' We've got some dynamite for 'em ourselves." The officer informed the judge of the threat, and Cox addressed that issue after the verdicts were read in court.

The following morning, October 20, 1967, the jury reached its decisions and was ready to give the judge its verdicts in the case of *U.S. v. Price, et al.* The foreman gave the sealed verdict to Cox, who read the paper and then gave it to the court clerk to read to the defendants. All the defendants stood as the verdicts were read in open court.

Seven men were found guilty by the jury: Cecil Ray Price, Jimmy Arledge, Sam Bowers, Wayne Roberts, Jimmy Snowden, Billy Wayne Posey, and Horace Doyle Barnette. Seven men were acquitted: Bernard Akin, Lawrence Rainey, Olen Burrage, Frank Herndon, Richard Willis, Herman Tucker, James Harris (the DOJ dropped charges against Travis Barnette, citing insufficient evidence to convict).

Three mistrials were declared by Judge Cox, including one for the organizer and planner of the killings, Preacher Killen, because the jurors could not reach a unanimous verdict. According to the jurors, there was a lone holdout regarding Killen's guilt or innocence. Evidently a female juror told her colleagues that "she could never convict a preacher." She held out, and a mistrial was declared by Cox.

"Damn her," said a fellow juror, seventy-six-year-old Nell Dedeaux, in May 2000, to a *Jackson Clarion-Ledger* news reporter. "I know the Preacher was guilty. He got away with it." From a photograph of the group of jurors, Dedeaux identified the lone holdout as Willie Arnesen, a Meridian secretary who died earlier in 2000. All the jurors contacted by the newspaper identified her as the sole holdout. One juror remembered her words in the jury room: "I'm not going to find Brother Killen guilty. I don't believe it. He wouldn't do such a thing. I'll stay here till Christmas!" Much later, Arnesen found out about Killen and told her son that "she was sorry she let him go."

Cox informed the seven convicted men of the bond and sentencing procedures and excused them — except for Cecil Price and Wayne Roberts. He announced that they would not be free on bond but would instead spend the weekend in jail because of Roberts's "dynamite" remark to Price in the court hallway the previous day:

> If you think you can intimidate this court, you are as badly mistaken as you can be. I'm not going to let any wild man loose on a civilized society and I want you locked up. I don't think you have taken this thing very seriously, and I'm going to give you an opportunity to think very seriously about it. I very heartily endorse the verdict of this jury. Particularly adjudging Mr. Roberts as guilty.

Bill Minor, covering the trial for the *New Orleans Times-Picayune*, summed up the importance of the guilty verdicts: "Never in this century has any white man in Mississippi been known to have been convicted and sent to prison for a federal civil rights violation." Until the guilty verdicts were announced, he observed, "the nation expected that a [white] Mississippi jury would allow the crimes to go unpunished." After all, the public had seen how white juries acquitted the two men who brutally murdered Emmett Till in 1955, the men who murdered Mack Charles Parker in 1959, as well as the murderer of NAACP's Mississippi field secretary, Medgar Evers, in 1963. In addition, there had been numerous murders of black civil rights workers that never led to indictments in state courts.

Judge Cox meted out the sentences. Although he was a stern jurist at the trial, no one believed that he had changed his racist views. Only two of the guilty men — Sam Bowers and Wayne Roberts — received the harshest punishment: a ten-year prison sentence. And the judge evidently tipped off defense lawyers that he would be very lenient when sentencing time came around. According to Sovereignty Commission investigator Hopkins's report of October 27, 1967, Judge Cox told Cecil Price's lawyer that his client should "wait until after the defendant was sentenced and that then he might not want to appeal the case."

The longest sentence imposed by Cox — for Bowers and Roberts — was ten years. The others received either a six-year or a three-year sentence. Actual time served by all but Roberts was not more than six years in a federal prison.

"They killed one nigger, one Jew, and a white man [*sic*]. I gave them all what I thought they deserved," Judge Cox commented after sentencing the seven Klansmen.

Responses after the Verdicts and the Sentencing

The *New York Times* headline on Saturday read, "Mississippi Jury Convicts 7 of 18 in Rights Killings." The reporter, Walter Rugaber, had covered the case since 1965 and had the pleasure of writing the story that closed a chapter on the grievous wrong perpetrated on three young men. His story described a surreal scene: "Philadelphia appeared rather subdued after news of the verdicts reached them. [However], the Central High School homecoming day parade, led by a 96-piece band in black and white uniforms, circled the courthouse square this afternoon."

The *New York Times* editorial the day after the verdicts were announced expressed the hope that the "verdicts were a measure of the quiet revolution that is taking place in Southern attitudes — a slow, still faltering, but inexorable conversion to the concept that a single standard of justice must cover whites and Negroes alike."

For almost two months after the verdicts were read in court, U.S. Marshals guarded the homes of all the jurors. Even before they reached their judgments in the case, U.S. Marshals told the group that one of the defendants said: "We've got dynamite for them if they find us guilty."

During the trial, the marshals were telephoned at home and threatened by Klansmen. The jury foreman, Langdon Anderson, also received such calls, including one that he received less than an hour after arriving at his home. The caller said, "It's important that certain things be done." Anderson knew the caller to be a Klansman and told his son who it was just in case something happened to him. "For a long time after the trial," said Anderson's son, "my dad always checked under the hood to make sure nothing was planted there."

At least four crosses were burned in Lumberton and Poplarville, the hometowns of two jurors. "The general consensus," said Anderson's son, "was that they were trial-related and were warnings."

Juror Nell Dedeaux, from Poplarville, Mississippi, a nurse with six children, was grateful for the protection. She told reporter Jerry Mitchell of the *Jackson Clarion-Ledger* that she "wasn't scared until I got home. I realized then there could be repercussions. With a bunch of crazies you didn't know what they might do. It was a time to be uneasy." When she arrived home, she immediately told her daughter's first-grade teachers not to let the young girl leave school with anybody else.

Another juror, Edsell Parks, of Brandon, Mississippi, recalled how the U.S. Marshals hid outside his house: "Those were bad times. I didn't expect them to come a-shooting, but you never know." Juror Lessie Lowery of Waynesboro, Mississippi, received threatening phone calls from unnamed men and was criticized for her decision by her neighbors. There was, however, a positive result of the threats she received: "Until I was threatened, a lot of people couldn't understand why I voted like I did."

Sam Bowers, the Mississippi Klan's Imperial Wizard, one of the seven found guilty, said to a reporter in 1983 (the statement found its way into print in a *Jackson Clarion-Ledger* story in 1998): "I was quite delighted to be convicted and have the main instigator of the entire affair [Preacher Killen] walk out of the courtroom a free man. Everybody, including the trial judge and the prosecutors and everybody else knows that that happened."

Another Klansman acquitted by the jury, Sheriff Lawrence Rainey, was nevertheless bitter and angry about the federal intruders. "The damn FBI was paying all the witnesses to lie. I attended some of the Klan meetings. They had open meetings, but that was all," he argued.

Deputy Sheriff Cecil Price, one of the seven Klansmen convicted of conspiracy, went back to work as a Neshoba County law enforcement officer immediately after the verdicts were announced. According to the Sovereignty Commission report, "Price was informed by Judge Cox that he saw no reason why he should not continue his employment as Chief Deputy Sheriff of Neshoba County and Price is still working in this capacity."

Price was also a candidate for sheriff in the Democratic primary but was defeated by Hop Barnett, who was also under indictment (but was one of three defendants about whom the jurors were unable to make a decision). And Wayne Roberts, the trigger man in the killings, "seems to be taking the matter as a joke," wrote Hopkins in his October 27, 1967, report to the commission.

Many, though not all, residents of Neshoba County were crestfallen when the verdicts were announced. According to the ubiquitous commission investigator A. L. Hopkins, "Most of the individuals that I heard talking [in Philadelphia] expressed surprise that some of the defendants were found guilty of this charge." Mississippi state officials barely supported the verdicts. Governor Paul Johnson said, "I feel that no one should argue with a jury." The state's attorney general, Joe Patterson, told reporters, "After all the criticism which has been directed against the state and its people, I think it is pertinent to point out that it was a Mississippi judge who presided over the federal court case, a Mississippi U.S. attorney who helped prosecute, and a Mississippi jury which convicted seven men."

Rita Schwerner-Bender, Mickey's wife, was somewhat relieved that the killers had not gotten off scot-free but was disappointed that no murder charges have been filed by the state since 1964. "It is past time for the State of Mississippi to fully investigate and acknowledge responsibility for these murders," she wrote in a 2000 letter to Philadelphia, Mississippi, District Attorney Ken Taylor.

J. E. Chaney's mother, who moved to New York City after her son's murder and after receiving threats to her life, told reporters, "They did better than I thought they would do."

Martin Luther King Jr. told a reporter that he was "pleasantly surprised." He saw the seven convictions "as a first step in a thousand-mile journey toward the goal of the equal administration of justice in Mississippi."

Forty days after the verdicts were rendered in the *Price* trial, John Doar retired from the DOJ and returned to the private practice of law. "It [is] the right time," he said. "I've been here [in the South] for seven years." Three decades later, Doar told a reporter, "We weren't trying to be heroes. At the same time, all of us realized that when our lives were almost over we wanted to be able to look back and say, 'we did our best: we worked as hard and as long as we could.'"

On December 29, 1967, Judge Cox sentenced the defendants, who immediately appealed their sentences to the Fifth Circuit U.S. Court of Appeals, in New Orleans, Louisiana. In July 1969, the appeals court upheld the sentences. The defense then filed a petition for certiorari with the U.S. Supreme Court. On February 27, 1970, the Court denied certiorari. Finally, on March 19, 1970, the seven Klansmen, having exhausted all their appeals, entered federal prisons across the nation, from Connecticut to Washington State.

CHAPTER 7

Is There Justice in Mississippi?

The past is never dead. It's not even past.

WILLIAM FAULKNER, INTRUDER IN THE DUST

By the middle of the 1970s, six of the seven convicted Klansmen had returned home to Mississippi to resume their ordinary lives. The sole exception was Wayne Roberts, the killer of the three civil rights workers, who served his full ten-year sentence in a federal penitentiary. No other action has been taken by the State of Mississippi to bring charges against the men who had been acquitted in the federal trial; no further action has been taken against any of the men whose trials ended in mistrial because of a deadlocked jury.

After Release from Federal Prison

What happened to the eighteen men after the 1967 trial? For nearly all of them, "life has hardly changed," wrote Jerry Mitchell, a reporter for the *Jackson Clarion-Ledger*, in 2000. They live in the same small towns, and most have the same telephone numbers they had in the 1960s. However, age has taken its toll; in 2001, fewer than half of the eighteen Klansmen charged with conspiring to murder Mickey Schwerner, J. E. Chaney, and Andy Goodman were still alive. Those who were alive were growing old and infirm; Preacher Killen was seventy-five years old in 2000.

Sam Bowers served six years of his ten-year sentence at McNeil Island in Washington State. In 1976 he resumed management of his Sambo Amusement Company in Laurel, Mississippi, continuing to do so until 1998, when he was sentenced to life imprisonment for the 1966 murder of NAACP leader Vernon Dahmer. Bowers is seventy-eight and serving his sentence at the Central Mississippi Correctional Facility in Rankin County.

Deputy Sheriff Cecil Ray Price served four years of his six-year sentence in the Federal Correctional Institution at Sandstone, Minnesota. After his release in 1974, he returned to Philadelphia, Mississippi, and held a number of jobs, including watch repairman, and then worked at the Olen Burrage Trucking Company. In a 1977 interview in the *New York Times*, he said he enjoyed watching *Roots* on television. He said his views about integration had changed: "We've got to accept this is the way things are going to be and that's it." He joined the local all-white country club when he returned to Philadelphia. In 1996 he was elected vice-president of the Neshoba County Shriners. He died in 2001 after a fall from a cherry picker.

Wayne Roberts, the brutal triggerman who killed the three men, served his ten years at the federal prison in Leavenworth, Kansas. He, too, returned home to Meridian, Mississippi, where he became a car salesman. He died in 1999.

Billy Wayne Posey was sentenced to six years at a federal prison in Atlanta, Georgia. He returned to Lauderdale County to manage a convenience store in the black community in Meridian. He later worked at a car dealership. He is retired and living in Meridian.

Jimmy Arledge was sentenced to a three-year term in the federal facility in Texarkana, Texas, where he was severely beaten by black prisoners. He finished his sentence in the Federal Youth Center in Ashland, Kentucky. He returned to Meridian, where he presently resides.

Jimmy Snowden was sentenced to a three-year term in Texas. He, too, was beaten by black inmates. He returned to Neshoba County, were he still lives.

Horace Doyle Barnette was sentenced to three years at a federal prison in Danbury, Connecticut. After serving his sentence, he moved to Louisiana and hoped-for anonymity. For years, however, he received threatening calls from the Klansmen whose names he had given to the FBI in 1964. As recently as 1993, "he would get threatening phone calls. That's something that's never gone away. He was very much an outcast." He died in 2001.

Preacher Killen never served a day for his critically important planning and organizational work in the deaths of Schwerner, Chaney, and Goodman. In 1976 he did wind up in state prison for five months for threatening a woman over the phone in 1974. He still lives in Union, Mississippi — a tiny town just south of Philadelphia — and runs a lumber mill that employs a number of black workers. He still preaches on

Sundays and still argues that God supports separation of the races. He is still a bitter, angry segregationist. He told a reporter in 2000, "I have no rights. I have to be a newspaper reporter or a nigger if I want to have rights."

E. G. "Hop" Barnett was reelected sheriff of Neshoba County while on trial in 1967. Because of a hung jury, he never served a day for his involvement in the murders. He drowned in the Pearl River in a fishing accident in 1989.

Jerry Sharpe, because of a hung jury, never served time in federal prison. After suffering a number of strokes and going blind, he died in March 2001.

Sheriff Lawrence Rainey, who was acquitted in 1967, never worked in law enforcement after the trial. He moved to Kentucky and then back to Meridian, where he found employment as a private security guard — working for a black boss, the Reverend Evan McDonald. In an ironic twist, McDonald resigned from his church, the Golden Grove Missionary Baptist Church, rather than fire Rainey — as his parishioners demanded. Rainey, too, still lives in Lauderdale County, suffering from throat cancer (due to his lifelong habit of chewing tobacco).

Richard Willis, the Philadelphia policeman, was also acquitted. He returned to police work and retired, living in adjacent Noxapater County.

Olen Burrage, whose property was used to bury the dead men, was acquitted. He still lives on the same site in Neshoba County.

Herman Tucker was found not guilty by the jury and lived out his life in Philadelphia. He died in March 2001.

Travis Barnette was also acquitted and lives in Mississippi.

Frank Herndon, the man who was accompanied by a nurse at the trial — was acquitted. He continued to reside in Meridian until he died.

James "Pete" Harris was acquitted. He still lives in Meridian.

Bernard Akin was also acquitted. He lived in Meridian until his death in 1986.

The three Klansmen (although two, Miller and Dennis, quit the Klan and were used as informants) who testified against the eighteen defendants fared little better after the trial ended. James Jordan, in a federal court in Georgia, was sentenced to four years for his part in the killing of the three men. After he served his time, he was relocated by the FBI to McClanney, Florida, where he worked in a funeral home. He died in 2000.

Delmar Dennis died on June 1, 1996. He was eulogized in the *New American* of July 22, 1996, the voice of the John Birch Society. In the article, "The Passing of an American Hero," the author, William Norman Grigg, noted that Dennis "displayed the purest form of heroism living a life of solitary commitment to Christian truth and the preservation of American liberty." After testifying in the 1967 trial, Dennis

> quickly found himself vilified by Klan sympathizers in his community. The pressures and anxieties of his undercover life also exacted a toll on his family. Fearing that her husband's actions might inspire retaliatory violence against their children, Dennis' wife divorced him. On several occasions attempts were made on his life. He was forced to discontinue his ministry. [However,] in 1968 he toured the country as a representative of the John Birch Society, describing the Klan's role in the plot to undermine American liberty.

In 1970, Dennis moved back to Mississippi as a John Birch Society coordinator. He died in his home state, said Grigg, "a Christian patriot who toiled in his lonely struggle for justice."

Wallace Miller is dead as well, survived by his widow, Nell Miller. She has spoken to the Mississippi attorney general, Mike Moore, about what she heard when Killen and her husband discussed eliminating Schwerner.

————

1990s: Belated Justice for Some Old Klan Killers

I have already noted the reality that, three decades after some brutal murders of civil rights workers and innocent bystanders, a number of southern states have successfully retried individuals accused of those criminal acts. When the crimes were committed, the perpetrators were rarely punished, much less indicted by local officials for their criminal actions. In the 1960s the state trials of the Klansmen who killed Mrs. Viola Liuzzo (a white civil rights volunteer involved in the 1965 Selma, Alabama, protest march) and Byron de la Beckwith, accused killer of Medgar Evers, ended with hung juries and declared mistrials. In the slaying of Colonel Lemuel Penn in Georgia, Herbert

Guest and the other Klansmen were acquitted by a state jury, even though one of the men confessed to the murder.

The trials of the accused killers of the Reverend James Reeb, another participant in the 1965 Selma, Alabama, march, a Unitarian minister from Washington, D.C., whose parishioners included the wife and daughter of U.S. Supreme Court Justice Hugo L. Black, as well as the retrial of the Liuzzo killers also ended in acquittals. In Mississippi, the state never charged any of the eighteen Klansmen with the murders of Schwerner, Chaney, and Goodman. Between 1960 and 1965, across the Deep South, only one man, Wayne Roberts, ever served a full sentence — ten years — for conspiring to take the lives of the three civil rights workers.

By the early 1990s, however, things had changed somewhat across the South. As of 2000, eighteen murder cases involving Klansmen and civil rights workers had been reopened by state prosecutors. In Alabama, in 2000, two former Klansmen, Bobby Frank Cherry and Tommy Blanton, both in their sixties, were indicted on murder charges for the 1963 killing of four black girls attending Sunday school classes in Birmingham's Sixteenth Street Baptist Church. Both men were convicted.

In 1999, in Louisiana's Washington Parish, a local prosecutor reopened the case of a 1965 ambush and shooting of the first black deputy sheriff in the parish. And in November 1999, a jury in Humphrey County, Mississippi, convicted three Klansmen of first-degree manslaughter in the 1970 murder of Rodney Pool, a one-armed sharecropper they threw into a river. In early 2000, also in Louisiana, the FBI reopened an investigation into the deaths of two black men found in a swamp in 1964. In 1998, in Mississippi, former Imperial Wizard Sam Bowers was convicted of ordering the bombing and death of NAACP leader Vernon Dahmer Sr. in 1966.

These unresolved criminal cases, ironically, are easier to deal with in 2000 than they were in the 1960s and 1970s, when the Klan was a much more forceful oppressor; it was not very difficult for a Klan leader such as Bowers to issue at least nine "Number 4" orders in three years (1964–1967). Juries in the 1960s, as already noted, were always all-white cohorts, with many of those serving as jurors Klansmen, former Klansmen, or members of the WCC. Invariably, the jurors practiced, crudely, "juror nullification" decades before the O.J.

Simpson trial. According to one observer writing in the *Economist* in 2000, the momentum for reexamining these unpunished murders from the height of the civil rights battles between the Klan and the civil rights groups "comes from a defiant group of young lawyers and prosecutors determined to discover the truth before time erodes the evidence or puts the suspects beyond reach."

A major fighter for justice in Mississippi is former (Democratic) Mississippi secretary of state Dick Molpus. In his early fifties, he is a native Philadelphia, Mississippi, resident whose family fought the Klan in its halcyon years, the 1960s. When his father, the owner of a prosperous sawmill in this piney woods area of the state, was threatened by the Klan because he hired black workers, Molpus recalled to Donna Ladd, he responded "by hiring three or four of the meanest guys in Neshoba County and giving them guns. He fought fire with fire."

Molpus, along with the state's fifty-year-old attorney general, Mike Moore, and Neshoba County's prosecuting attorney, thirtyish Ken Turner, believes that the state must bring murder charges against those Klansmen still living who were involved in the June 1964 slaying of Schwerner, Chaney, and Goodman. He recently observed, "There are lots of people with good hearts in that town, but a lot just wish it would go away. But it's a pall on the county; it will never go away, or diminish if justice is never served."

Although these men know the difficulties that lie in the path of such a decision, they, in the words of Dick Molpus, "love the fight here. It's a worthy scrap." As of the present time, however, the "scrap" has not taken place.

The Renewed Cry for Justice from the Families of the Dead Civil Rights Workers

In 1989, Dick Molpus did something no other Mississippi official had ever done, and no politician has done since. He publicly apologized for the murders of Schwerner, Chaney, and Goodman during a memorial service marking the twenty-fifth anniversary of the deaths of the three men. At a ceremony in Longdale, the black section of Philadelphia, adjacent to the Mount Zion Methodist Church, in front of the families of the three dead men, he said:

This is an appropriate opportunity to apologize to the parents, siblings, and spouse of Mssrs. Chaney, Schwerner, and Goodman. We deeply regret what happened here twenty-five years ago. We wish we could undo it. We are profoundly sorry they are gone. We wish we could bring them back. Every decent person in Philadelphia and Neshoba County feels exactly the same way.

In Molpus's unsuccessful run for Mississippi governor in 1995, his opponent, Republican candidate Kirk Fordice, rebuked him for apologizing to the families of the dead civil rights workers in 1989, saying that it did "no good" to drag up the past. "I don't believe," he said, "we need to keep running this state by 'Mississippi Burning' and apologizing for thirty years ago. This is the nineties! This is now! We're on a roll. We've got the best race relations in America, and we need to speak positive Mississippi! We have the most black elected officials in the nation! That's Mississippi!" Molpus responded, "I apologized then, and I make no apology to you about it." Molpus, however, lost the November election, receiving only 40 percent of the votes, whereas Fordice received 60 percent.

Rita Schwerner Bender heard Molpus's words in 1989 and renewed her struggle to get the state to try the Klansmen for murder in state court. Although remarried and living in Seattle, Washington, she has worked ceaselessly since then to see that event take place in Mississippi. In 2002, she said, "I believe there should be a trial so there is public recognition of the state and the individuals who didn't want to get their hands dirty in the reign of terror. The reason I think it's important is so that we can teach our children and grandchildren what can happen if government is complicit."

Andy Goodman's mother, Carolyn Goodman, agreed with Rita Bender. "It's like having something hang over your head. There should be a closing. There should be a trial. I'm not looking for blood, but I think some decision has to be made as to the guilt of whoever is left," she said to a reporter in 2002.

J. E. Chaney's brother Ben said that the killers have not yet been punished. "The perpetrators are walking the streets, and we all know who they are. By not prosecuting, it's saying to the individuals, 'You can go home and tell your friends about it, and nothing will be done.'"

Lawrence Guyot was the last black person to see the three men alive. He spoke with them when they visited the burned-out Mount Zion Methodist Church on Father's Day, June 21, 1964, and testified to that effect at the federal conspiracy trial in 1967. He said to a *Clarion-Ledger* reporter in 2002, "It's never too late to do what's right."

In 1999, as a result of continued pressure and the release by the FBI of more than 40,000 files pertaining to the case, Attorney General Mike Moore reopened the case. Working with Ken Turner, the district attorney of Neshoba County, the duo decided that it was time to deal with the past. Like Molpus, Turner is a Philadelphia native (he also is a cousin of the late *New York Times* executive editor, Turner Catledge). The district attorney said, "I realize it's been an albatross around our neck for 36 years. It'd be nice to get it off." As he told reporter Donna Ladd in 2001, however, he would only bring a strong case into court: "It's not fair to throw a [weak] case out there, and say, 'well, we tried.' . . . That would be more harmful. I'd take the heat for that."

Moore had just concluded his successful fight against the major tobacco companies, and in 1997 the *National Law Review* named him "Lawyer of the Year." When the film *The Insider* was made about the events, Moore played himself.

Moore said that he was considering filing murder charges against the Klan conspirators who took the lives of Schwerner, Chaney, and Goodman in 1964, especially the organizer, Preacher Killen. As Moore said to a *Newsweek* reporter in June 2000, "My message to Preacher Killen is if I can make a case, you're going to be the first to be indicted."

Moore, however, faced a big problem. Many of the Klansmen were dead, including the men who had testified against them in 1967, Delmar Dennis, Wallace Miller, and Jim Jordan. To bring a case into state court, Moore said that he had to persuade some of the living conspirators to become witnesses for the prosecution. In 2002, there were only nine living suspects in the proposed murder case against the killers of the civil rights workers: Bowers (already serving a life sentence for the murder of Vernon Dahmer), Arledge, Snowden, Posey, Rainey, Willis, Harris, Burrage, and the Preacher, Edgar Ray Killen.

Moore had a number of conversations with former deputy sheriff Price about the law enforcement officer testifying as a witness for the prosecution. However, in 2001, Price died unexpectedly after falling twenty feet from a cherry picker while working at a heavy equipment rental company. After Price's death, a disappointed Moore said that Price had been the state's best witness because he had told Moore everything that took place the evening of June 21, 1964. According to Moore, "We were going to get indictments against one defendant, if not more. When Cecil Price died, it took a lot of wind out of our sails." His primary focus was on Edgar Ray "Preacher" Killen. However, when asked which of the Klansmen who were still alive might be charged with murder, he said:

> All of them, The way the kids were killed is as mean a crime as I know about — killing for no other purpose than to kill them. These three kids believed in what they were doing, and they were brutally murdered. I think about how fearful they were. With police and a gang of thugs, they just ripped them out of the car, shooting them and beating them. That's just mean.

Moore was not deterred: "We're looking for any new witnesses, new leads, new strategies, and new information."

By 2002, three new witnesses were prepared to testify against the Klansmen who killed Schwerner, Chaney, and Goodman. Bob Stringer was a teenager when Bowers issued orders to Killen for the murder of Schwerner. Ernest Gilbert, a former Klansmen who became an FBI informant, was present when Killen planned another murder just weeks before June 21, 1964. And George Metz, a retired investigator, has told Moore that Killen admitted to cleaning the murder scene the morning after the killing.

Moore is still optimistic and believes that there was a major benefit in reopening the murder case: "Maybe by doing this old case, we'll change some of those old stereotypes [about Mississippi]." On the thirty-eighth anniversary of the deaths of the three civil rights workers, he told the press, "We're never going to give up on this case because we think it's important."

Not everyone in Mississippi looks forward to such a state criminal trial. Not everyone thinks the case is "important." Scott Johnson, a young lawyer in Philadelphia, Mississippi, argues that opening the case is just another "political tool" for politicians such as Mike Moore. "In 2000 to date," he told writer Donna Ladd, "there are unsolved murders in Jackson, in Meridian. What makes one death more important than another death? What are their motives [for reopening the case]?" Johnson believes that the attorney general is using the case "as a hot button to get media attention and a cameo role [for himself] when the movie comes out."

However, there seems to be a change in attitudes about the importance of having charges brought against the Klansmen. The *Neshoba Democrat*, the county's once-rabidly segregationist weekly, editorialized in May 2000: "Come hell or high water, it's time for an accounting."

2004 — The Still Unanswered Question: Is There Justice in Mississippi?

One of my very good students when I taught political science at Mississippi State University in the 1970s was Sid Salter, who grew up in Philadelphia, Mississippi. In 2003, more than two decades later, he is the features editor at the *Jackson Clarion-Ledger*. In May 2001, he was the editor and publisher of the *Scott County Times*, but wrote a column, entitled "Price's Death Doesn't Dispel State's Ghosts," for the *Clarion Ledger* about the death of Cecil Ray Price. The column was a powerful statement written by a Mississippian about the death of his neighbor and the father of one of Salter's Philadelphia friends.

Salter pointed out that while Price's dying meant his escape from a possible murder charge, "for anyone to suggest that Price never suffered for his crime beyond the six-year federal prison term is absurd in the extreme":

> From the time he returned to Neshoba County in 1974, Price lived the rest of his life like an insect on a pin under the scrutiny of entomologists. His family suffered with him. . . . There remain some in Mississippi who would defend Cecil Price for his actions in the 1960's and who delight in the fact that he through death has now escaped state prosecution for his crimes. . . . [While] Cecil Price has settled up, it's time that the state of Mississippi finally admits in a state court that three youths were murdered by a lynch mob some 37 years ago in Neshoba County and sets about to punish the guilty — no matter who they are. Price's death sets even more clearly into focus the need to get this case in front of a Neshoba County grand jury in 2001.

Another excellent former student of mine at Mississippi State University, writer, journalist, and poet Donna Ladd, also grew up in Philadelphia, Mississippi. She and her mother would regularly visit Cecil Price — after he served his time in prison — in the jewelry store in their town where he worked. "I always liked Cecil Price," Ladd wrote in 2000. "My first memories of the man-with-an-extra-eye fall sometime in the early 1970's when I first began developing an interest in jewelry."

> He would look up from the watch he seemed to be dissecting. As his eyes focused on me and then my mother, he would break into his jolly, mischievous grin, the same one I would later see in the library's archives. "Howdy, Katie Mae, Donna Kay. What you got for me?" . . . I had no idea one of the more notorious racists in the country was doctoring my Timex and resetting my birthstone ring.

After graduating from Mississippi State University, Ladd left the state for a career in journalism in New York City (writing for the *Village Voice* and other news weeklies and receiving a graduate degree in journalism from Columbia University) and in Denver, Colorado. However, like many young expatriate Mississippians, in 2002 she came back to her state and is presently practicing her craft in the state capital, Jackson.

In a recent essay, "Letter from Mississippi: It's about Race, Stupid!" Ladd reflected on the events that took place in June 1964— and looked at the Mississippi of 2001.

> Yesterday I stood in the spot where my Neshoba County neighbors executed Jim Chaney, Andy Goodman, and Mickey Schwerner 37 years ago last month. It was over 100 degrees in Mississippi just like it was June 21, 1964. Stepping out of an air-conditioned car three-tenths of a mile off Highway 19 South on what the FBI called Rock Creek Road, I felt dizzy and slightly nauseous when the Dixie humidity hit my forehead. . . . There is no memorial on the patch of Mississippi road where otherwise "good" family men played out a brutal, shameful, cowardly murder plan on behalf of the state's white majority. . . . Neshoba County has not apologized. It has not yet tried its murderers, although the case is open again. A memorial there probably wouldn't make it through the first night, said my escort, a

Mississippian who never left, who has fought my hometown's bigotry for the last 33 years, who yearns for closure. I nodded sadly: He's right, I know.

A plaque located next to the rebuilt Mount Zion Methodist Church is dedicated to the memory of the three young men who were murdered in June 1964. It reads:

> On June 21, 1964, voting rights activists James Chaney, Andrew Goodman, and Michael Schwerner, who had come here to investigate the burning of Mount Zion church, were murdered. Victims of a Klan conspiracy, their deaths provoked national outrage and led to the first successful prosecution of a civil rights case in Mississippi.

For Mississippians living in Neshoba County, for the thousands of folk living in Philadelphia, Mississippi, the past will remain with them until justice is done. It is past time for a final accounting. Cold-blooded murder was committed in Neshoba County on the night of June 21, 1964. There cannot be any peace or rest until justice is done.

CHRONOLOGY

1964

January 15	Bob Moses, COFO leader, announces the 1964 "Mississippi Freedom Summer" project to register blacks to vote.
February 1	Mickey Schwerner and his wife, Rita, already in Meridian, Mississippi, in Lauderdale County, formally head up the Meridian, Mississippi, CORE office.
February 15	The founding meeting of the White Knights of the Ku Klux Klan of Mississippi takes place.
May 30	Schwerner and James Chaney, another CORE worker, speak at Mount Zion Methodist Church in Neshoba County about voter registration and the possibility of using the church as a voter registration training center.
June 14	Andy Goodman and hundreds of other student volunteers for the Mississippi Freedom Summer project arrive in Oxford, Ohio, for their weeklong training program prior to their departure for Mississippi towns. Attending this program are Schwerner and Chaney, among the two dozen CORE/COFO civil rights "veterans."
June 16–17	Lauderdale and Neshoba County Klansmen assault leaders of Mount Zion Church and then burn the church to the ground, one of dozens of black Mississippi churches burned during the summer of 1964.
June 17	The FBI begins an investigation into church bombings in Mississippi, code-named "MIBURN," for "Mississippi Burning."
June 20	Schwerner, Chaney, and Andy Goodman, who volunteered to work in Meridian office, drive from Ohio to the CORE office in Meridian, Mississippi.
June 21	The three men drive to the site of the burned Mount Zion Methodist Church. On their return to Meridian, they are stopped in Philadelphia by Deputy Sheriff Price for allegedly speeding and are brought to the county jail in town. Six hours later, around 10:30 P.M., they are released after paying a twenty-dollar speeding fine. They

return to Highway 19 south to Meridian. A few miles outside Philadelphia, their Ford station wagon is overtaken by Sheriff Price, who brings them to a waiting group of Klansmen. They are taken to a dirt road off the highway and shot to death. Their bodies are buried in an earthen dam miles away.

June 22	The FBI begins its investigation into the disappearance of the trio. Joseph Sullivan is designated the Special Agent in Charge of the investigation.
June 23	The FBI locates the trio's charred station wagon in the Bogue Chitto Swamp, thirteen miles northeast of Philadelphia.
June 23	President Lyndon Baines Johnson meets with U.S. Attorney General Robert Kennedy and others to plan the administration's response to the emergent crisis in Mississippi.
July 10	FBI Director J. Edgar Hoover opens the Mississippi office of the FBI in Jackson, Mississippi.
July 31	The FBI learns of the probable location of the bodies of the three civil rights workers.
August 3	The FBI receives a search warrant to look for bodies in an earthen dam at the Old Jolly farm outside Philadelphia.
August 4	The bodies of the three men are found buried between fifteen and seventeen feet deep in the earthen dam.
September	A federal grand jury does not indict twenty-one Klansmen. The state defers bringing Klansmen before a state grand jury charging defendants with murder of the three civil rights workers.
October 13	Klansman James Jordan confesses his involvement in the Klan conspiracy to murder the trio to the FBI and agrees to cooperate with the bureau's investigators.
November 19	Klansman Horace Barnette confesses and describes the shootings to the FBI.
October–November	The FBI refuses to turn information over to the Neshoba County prosecutor for use by the state to possibly indict persons for the murders of the three civil rights workers. The state does not bring criminal charges against Klansmen.

| December 4 | Twenty-one suspects in the Klan conspiracy to murder the trio are arrested and nineteen charged with violating the civil rights of Schwerner, Chaney, and Goodman (18 *U.S.C.* Sections 241 and 242). |
| December 10 | U.S. Commissioner Esther Carter dismisses the charges against the nineteen men because the FBI presented the Barnette confession rather than producing Horace Barnette in person in the courtroom. |

1965

January 10	A federal grand jury in Jackson, Mississippi, indicts eighteen men for the murders of the civil rights trio.
January 15	The FBI arrests eighteen men; most were arrested in December 1964
February 25–26	U.S. District Court Judge Harold Cox dismisses indictments — except for those for Sheriff Lawrence Rainey, Deputy Sheriff Cecil Price, and Philadelphia policeman Richard Willis — on grounds that conspirators were not acting "under color of law" — murder is not a federal crime and that only the three law enforcement officers can be tried under 18 *U.S.C.* 242.
April	U.S. Supreme Court denies request from federal government in *U.S. v. Price* to hear appeal on an "expedited basis" but sets dates for submission of briefs and oral arguments on jurisdiction and on the merits.

1966

| March 28 | U.S. Supreme Court unanimously reverses the Cox decision and reinstates the original indictments against the eighteen conspirators. |
| October 7 | Judge Cox again dismisses indictments, agreeing with defense attorneys, who claimed that the pool of potential jurors did not include enough minorities and women. |

1967

| February 28 | The nineteen men are again indicted, by another federal grand jury, for conspiring to murder the trio. Jordan's case, however, separated and moved to another state (because he was a prosecution witness). |

October 9	The trial begins in U.S. District Court, Judge Harold Cox presiding.
October 12	Jordan testifies about the murders of the three civil rights workers.
October 18	The case goes to the jury.
October 19	Deadlocked jury receives "Allen charge" from Judge Cox.
October 20	The jury finds seven defendants guilty. Seven defendants are acquitted, charges are dropped against one defendant, and the jury is unable to reach a verdict on three of the men charged with conspiracy.
December 29	Judge Cox sentences the seven convicted men to prison terms ranging from three to ten years.
1970	
March 19	The appeals exhausted, the seven men enter federal prisons across the country.
1998	
December 27	Families of Schwerner, Chaney, and Goodman call for reopening of the case when newspapers report that Sam Bowers, former Imperial Wizard of the Mississippi KKK (convicted in 1967 and sentenced to ten years in federal prison), admits that he evaded justice in the case, saying he did not mind going to prison because a fellow Klansman got away with murder.
1999	
February 25	Mississippi attorney general Mike Moore and Neshoba County district attorney Ken Turner meet to discuss opening a state investigation of the murders of the civil rights trio.
December	Moore's office receives more than 40,000 pages of data from the FBI on the case.
2000	
May 14	Bob Stringer, who worked for Bowers in the 1960s, says he overheard Bowers tell Preacher Killen to "eliminate" Mickey Schwerner.
2001	
May 6	Former deputy sheriff Cecil Price, who had begun working with state authorities investigating the trio's

murders, dies of injuries suffered from a twenty-foot fall from a cherry picker.

July 19   Retired investigator George Metz claims that Killen admitted cleaning the trio's murder scene the morning after they were killed.

2004   After forty years, there are still no state indictments of those who murdered Schwerner, Goodman, and Cheney.

RELEVANT CASES

Allen v. U.S., 164 U.S. 492 (1896)

Bolling v. Sharpe, 347 U.S. 497 (1954)

Briggs, et al. v. R. W. Elliott, 342 U.S. 350 (1954)

Brown v. Board of Education of Topeka, Kansas, 347 U.S. 485 (1954)

Brown v. Board of Education of Topeka, Kansas, 349 U.S. 294 (1955)

Civil Rights Cases, 109 U.S. 3 (1883)

Ex parte Yarbrough, 110 U.S. 651 (1884)

Gayle v. Browder, 352 U.S. 903 (1956)

Green v. County School Board of New Kent County, Virginia, 391 U.S. 430 (1968)

Guinn v. U.S., 238 U.S. 347 (1915)

Monroe v. Pape, 365 U.S. 167 (1961)

Morgan v. Virginia, 328 U.S. 373 (1946)

Plessy v. Ferguson, 163 U.S. 537 (1896)

Screws v. U.S., 325 U.S. 91 (1945)

Smith v. Allwright, 321 U.S. 649 (1944)

U.S. v. Cruikshank, et al., 92 U.S. 542 (1876)

U.S. v. Fordice, 505 U.S. 717 (1992)

U.S. v. Guest, et al., 383 U.S. 745 (1966)

U.S. v. Price, et al., 383 U.S. 787 (1966)

U.S. v. Williams, et al., 341 U.S. 70 (1951)

Walker v. Birmingham, 388 U.S. 307 (1967)

Williams, et al. v. U.S., 341 U.S. 97 (1951)

BIBLIOGRAPHICAL ESSAY

The story of the murders of Mickey Schwerner, J. E. Chaney, and Andy Goodman begins with an examination of the variety of original resources located in a number of states and the District of Columbia. For information about the views of the U.S. Supreme Court's justices about the validity of the post–Civil War statutes (18 *U.S.C.* 241, 242), the Library of Congress Manuscript Division was once again an invaluable place to work. There one can view the papers of Hugo L. Black, William J. Brennan, William O. Douglas, and Thurgood Marshall, and those of the "Super Chief," Earl Warren.

In addition, Associate Justice John M. Harlan II's papers, located in the Mudd Memorial Library at Princeton University, Princeton, New Jersey, are available to researchers. Justice Tom C. Clark's papers are found in the University of Texas Law Library in Austin, Texas. Columbia University's oral history collection provided an excellent transcript of Thurgood Marshall's views on the issues discussed in this book.

Presidential libraries were also of great value in the telling of the story of the civil rights workers' murders. The Dwight David Eisenhower Presidential Papers, in the Eisenhower Library, Abilene, Kansas; President John F. Kennedy's papers located in his library in Boston, Massachusetts; and the papers of President Lyndon Baines Johnson, found in the University of Texas's Special Collection Division, Austin, Texas, are excellent sources for insights into administrative responses to the growing crisis in the South in the 1950s and 1960s.

The Library of Congress contains the papers and documents of some of the civil rights organizations that participated in the Mississippi Freedom Summer project, in 1964. The Council of Federated Organization (COFO) Papers, the Congress of Racial Equality (CORE) Papers, and the records of the National Association for the Advancement of Colored People (NAACP) are open and available to interested persons. Obviously, these sources were invaluable in the writing of the book. So, too, were the Federal Bureau of Investigation (FBI) MIBURN files, located at www.law.umkc.edu/faculty/projects/trials/html.

Finally, thanks to a federal district court judge's order in 1998, the once-secret Mississippi State Sovereignty Commission Papers have become available to researchers. These materials are located in the Search Room of the Mississippi Department of Archives and History, in Jackson, Mississippi.

Special mention must be made of the wonderful work of Douglas O. Linder, a professor at the University of Missouri, Kansas City. He has created an excellent Web site that features original and secondary resource materials about important trials in American courts. The site includes the "Mississippi Burning: U.S. v Price Trial" Homepage, 2001, at www.law.umkc.edu/faculty/projects/

trials/html, which contains the FBI files as well as the transcripts of the October 1967 trial of the eighteen Klansmen charged with conspiring to take the Fourteenth Amendment rights of Schwerner, Chaney, and Goodman.

Materials from the following newspapers were helpful in the preparation of this book: the *New York Times*, the *Jackson Clarion-Ledger*, the *Jackson Daily News*, the *Neshoba Democrat*, the *Economist*, the *Washington Post*, the *Fort Worth Star-Telegram*, the *Pittsburgh Post-Gazette*, and the *New York Daily News*. Interesting, informative essays from these papers include: Note, "Southern History: Don't Forget," *Economist*, June 10, 2000; Joseph Lelyveld, "A Stranger in Philadelphia, Mississippi," *New York Times Sunday Magazine*, December 27, 1964; Paul Hendrickson, "Twenty Years Ago in the Heat of the Night," *Washington Post Magazine*, July 10, 1984; and Will Haygood, "A Mississippi Odyssey," *Washington Post Magazine*, September 29, 2002. David Nevin's story "A Strange, Tight Little Town, Loath to Admit Complicity," *Life*, December 18, 1964, was another piece of insightful reporting.

Especially acute reporting — containing a wealth of information — was exhibited in the series of articles by a *Clarion-Ledger* reporter, Jerry Mitchell, entitled "44 Days That Changed Mississippi," *Jackson Clarion-Ledger*, May 7, 2000–January 8, 2001. Mitchell did a masterful job of interviewing dozens of persons whose lives were dramatically and permanently affected by the events of June 21 and 22, 1964.

Donna Ladd's "Unfinished Business: Mississippi Struggles with Racist Past and Present" (master's thesis, Columbia University, 2000), presented the insights of a young person who grew up in Philadelphia, Mississippi, in the turbulent 1960s and 1970s. Other works written by persons who were there at the time include Florence Mars's book *Witness in Philadelphia* (Baton Rouge: Louisiana State University Press, 1977); and a book by James Silver, an Ole Miss professor of history, *Mississippi: The Closed Society* (New York: Harcourt, Brace, and World, 1963), which opened the state's xenophobia to the nation.

Other writers whose firsthand observations of 1960s Mississippi were invaluable include Charles Marsh, "Rendezvous with the Wizard," *Oxford American*, October/November 1996. His books *God's Long Summer: Stories of Faith and Civil Rights* (Princeton, N.J.: Princeton University Press, 1997), and *The Last Days: A Son's Story of Sin and Segregation at the Dawn of a New South* (New York: Basic Books, 2001) give intimate portraits of some of the key figures in Mississippi in that era. Mary Winstead's *Back to Mississippi: A Personal Journey through the Events That Changed America in 1964* (New York: Hyperion, 2002), is another well-written essay by a relative of "Preacher" Killen. Finally, James P. Turner's essay, "Police Accountability in the Federal System," *McGeorge Law Review* 30 (spring 1999): 991, provides a view of the era from the perspective of a leading figure in the DOJ's Civil Rights Division for almost three decades.

Civil rights advocates' books were also important sources. These include Len Holt, *The Summer That Didn't End: The Story of the Mississippi Civil Rights Project of 1964* (New York: William Morrow, 1965); Clayborne Carson, *In Struggle: SNCC and the Black Awakening of the 1960s* (Cambridge, Mass.: Harvard University Press, 1995); Charles Payne, *I've Got the Light of Freedom: The Organizing Tradition and the Mississippi Freedom Struggle* (Berkeley: University of California Press, 1995); James Farmer, *Lay Bare the Heart: An Autobiography of the Civil Rights Movement* (New York: Penguin, 1985); Kay Mills, *This Little Light of Mine: The Life of Fanny Lou Hamer* (New York: Penguin, 1993); Mary King, *Freedom's Song* (New York: Random House, 1987); Sally Belfrage, *Freedom Summer* (New York: Viking, 1965); and Robert Moses and Charles E. Cobb Jr., *Radical Equations* (Boston: Beacon Press, 2001).

A contrary view of the events in the South after the *Brown* decision came down in 1954 is presented in Tom Brady, *Black Monday* (Brookhaven, Miss.: White Citizens Council, 1954).

A number of anthologies focus, in part, on this era of civil rights history. These include Henry Hampton and Steve Fayer, ed., *Voices of Freedom: An Oral History of the Civil Rights Movement from the 1950s through the 1980s* (New York: Bantam Books, 1991); Terry H. Anderson, *The Movement and the Sixties* (New York: Oxford University Press, 1995); and Raymond D'Angelo, ed., *The American Civil Rights Movement: Readings and Interpretations* (Boston: McGraw-Hill/Dushkin, 2001).

Some major secondary sources relied upon by the author include Neil McMillan, *The Citizens' Council: Organizing Resistance to the Second Reconstruction* (Urbana: University of Illinois Press, 1971); John Dittmer, *Local People: The Struggle for Civil Rights in Mississippi* (Urbana: University of Illinois Press, 1994); Stephen J. Whitfield, *A Death in the Delta: The Story of Emmett Till* (Baltimore: Johns Hopkins University Press, 1988); Don Whitehead, *Attack on Terror: The FBI versus the Ku Klux Klan in Mississippi* (New York: Funk and Wagnalls, 1970); W. J. Cash, *The Mind of the South* (New York: Knopf, 1941; Vintage, 1991); Mary Aikin Rothschild, *A Case of Black and White: Northern Volunteers and the Southern Freedom Summers* (Westport, Conn.: Greenwood Press, 1982); Brian K. Landsberg, *Enforcing Civil Rights: Race Discrimination and the Department of Justice* (Lawrence: University Press of Kansas, 1997); John R. Howard, *The Shifting Wind: The Supreme Court and Civil Rights from Reconstruction to Brown* (Albany: State University of New York Press, 1999); David R. Goldfield, *Black, White and Southern: Race Relations and Southern Culture 1940 to the Present* (Baton Rouge: Louisiana State University Press, 1990); Donald G. Nieman, *Promises to Keep: African-Americans and the Constitutional Order, 1776 to the Present* (New York: Oxford University Press, 1991); Howard Ball and Phillip Cooper, *Of Power and Right: Justices Hugo Black, William O. Douglas and America's Constitutional Revolution* (New

York: Oxford University Press, 1992); Howard Ball, *A Defiant Life: Thurgood Marshall and the Persistence of Racism in American Life* (New York: Random House/Crown, 1999); Carl T. Rowan, *Dream Makers, Dream Breakers: The World of Justice Thurgood Marshall* (Boston: Little, Brown, 1993); Taylor Branch, *Parting the Waters: America during the King Years, 1954–1963* (New York: Simon and Schuster, 1989); William Bradford Huie, *Three Lives for Mississippi* (New York: White Citizens Council Books, 1964); Michael Belknap, "The Vindication of Burke Marshall: The Southern Legal System and the Anti–Civil Rights Violence of the 1960s," *Emory Law Journal* 33 (winter 1984): 93; Yasuhiro Katagiri, *The Mississippi State Sovereignty Commission: Civil Rights and States' Rights* (Jackson: University of Mississippi Press, 2001); Harris Wofford, *Of Kennedys and Kings: Making Sense of the Sixties* (Pittsburgh: University of Pittsburgh Press, 1980); and Michael Beschloss, ed., *Taking Charge: The Johnson White House Tapes, 1963–1964* (New York: Simon and Schuster, 1997).

Many hundreds of other books, monographs, and articles in law reviews and other professional journals have discussed this era of American social, political, and legal history. In addition, the Internet continues to be an *unlimited* source of information for all persons interested in civil rights in America in the violent decades of the mid–twentieth century. The enumeration of sources in this essay barely scratches the surface.

INDEX

{ *Murder in Mississippi* }